Twayne's English Authors Series

Sylvia E. Bowman, *Editor*

INDIANA UNIVERSITY

Henry Mackenzie

TEAS 184

Portrait by Sir Henry Raeburn,
photo courtesy of the National Portrait Gallery, London

Henry Mackenzie

Henry Mackenzie

By GERARD A. BARKER

Queens College of The City University of New York

TWAYNE PUBLISHERS

A DIVISION OF G. K. HALL & CO., BOSTON

Library of Congress Cataloging in Publication Data

Barker, Gerard A.
Henry Mackenzie.

(Twayne's English authors series)
Bibliography: pp. 185–86
Includes index.
1. Mackenzie, Henry, 1745–1831–Criticism and interpretation.
PR3543.M2Z63 823'.6 74–34318
ISBN 0-8057-6651-0

MANUFACTURED IN THE UNITED STATES OF AMERICA

For

Ann

Contents

About the Author

Gerard A. Barker is an Associate Professor of English at Queens College of the City University of New York. He received his B.A. from the University of California at Berkeley and his Ph.D. from Stanford University. A specialist in the eighteenth-century novel, Professor Barker is the author of essays on Samuel Richardson, Henry Mackenzie, Fanny Burney, William Godwin, and Jane Austen. His articles have been published in *Studies in English Literature* and the *Bulletin of the New York Public Library* and will soon appear in *Studies in the Novel* and *Papers on Language and Literature.* An essay on Shakespeare's *Pericles*, originally published in *English Studies*, has been reprinted in the Penguin anthology, *Shakespeare's Later Comedies.*

Preface

If the usual fate of minor writers is to become identified with a single work, Henry Mackenzie is a classic example of this phenomenon. Although he wrote two other novels, besides being an active playwright, essayist, and critic, he is remembered today almost exclusively as the author of *The Man of Feeling*. His third novel, *Julia de Roubigné*, though his best, is largely ignored and unread, as are his tales and critical essays, but three new editions of *The Man of Feeling* have appeared since 1958. A need clearly exists, it seems to me, to reassess Henry Mackenzie's achievement as a writer.

Limited as I am in length, I have focused my attention on his fiction, dramas, and literary criticism (three areas in which Mackenzie's effort has been substantial), although I have included, in the introductory biographical section, brief descriptions of his work as poet, periodical essayist, and man of letters. The four subsequent chapters are devoted to analyzing his novels and major tales chronologically, tracing his artistic development, and defining the intellectual background that helped to shape his themes and characterizations. In Chapter 6, Mackenzie's parallel growth as playwright is examined through an analysis of his three tragedies and his little-known comedy. Finally, in Chapter 7, his major critical essays are discussed, evaluated, placed in historical perspective, and related to his own novels and dramas.

A definitive study of the sentimental novel remains to be written, our knowledge of the genre being dependent upon a few pioneer works and historical surveys. Such a paucity of scholarship encourages facile assumptions and generalizations about a complex literary movement and often leads us to read individual works of fiction only to confirm preconceived notions about the sentimental novel. The present study is an attempt to correct such misconceptions, at least as far as they apply to Mackenzie, by subjecting him to the kind of critical scrutiny we normally reserve only for major writers.

Mackenzie, it seems to me, is particularly suited for such a purpose, since his attitude toward sensibility, especially as it finds expression in the moral and esthetic context of his novels, reflects not only his time but his singularly personal response to it. The Cult of Feeling swept much of Europe in the late decades of the eighteenth century, and its values obviously permeate his writings. Yet, although he reveres sensibility and endows most of his virtuous characters with it, one discerns in Mackenzie a growing awareness of its liabilities, an increasing realization that to be endowed with such acute emotional susceptibility was to be more easily led astray by one's own feelings or manipulated by the machinations of others. This recognition, running counter to his own inclination and temperament, gives his work its notable sense of ambivalence and its historical significance.

I wish to express my thanks to a number of persons and institutions. I am grateful to the Trustees of the National Library of Scotland and in particular to Mr. James Ritchie, Deputy Keeper of Manuscripts, for making the letters and papers of Mackenzie available to me and for permitting me to quote from them; to Professors Horst W. Drescher and Edgar Mertner as well as Verlag Aschendorff of Münster, West Germany, for allowing me to quote from *Henry Mackenzie, Letters to Elizabeth Rose of Kilravock*; to Professor Marion Thompson for allowing me to reprint excerpts from *The Anecdotes and Egotisms of Henry Mackenzie*, edited by her husband, the late Harold W. Thompson, to whom every student of Mackenzie is indebted; to the Pierpont Morgan Library for permission to quote from some Mackenzie correspondence; and to the Huntington Library, San Marino, California, for allowing me to quote from the manuscript of Mackenzie's *The Force of Fashion*, HM LA 852.

I would like to thank Mr. Robert B. Woodings for helpful suggestions during the writing of this study. For their constructive and judicious criticism of the manuscript, I am greatly indebted to my colleagues Professors Stanley Friedman, Robert A. Colby, and Vineta Colby. Finally, I would like to thank my wife, not only for her assistance in proofreading and indexing this book, but for her support and equanimity throughout its composition.

GERARD A. BARKER

Queens College of the City University of New York

Chronology

1745 Henry Mackenzie born August 6 (n.s.) in Edinburgh, son of a prominent physician.
1751 Entered Edinburgh High School.
1758 Entered Edinburgh University.
1759 Death of mother, Margaret Rose of Kilravock.
1761 Articled as clerk for five years to George Inglis, King's Attorney in Exchequer.
1763 "Happiness," first published poem, in the *Scots Magazine.*
1764 Ballad of "Duncan" published in the *Scots Magazine.*
1765 Ballad of "Kenneth" published in the *Scots Magazine.* Admitted attorney in Court of Exchequer of Scotland; went to London to study English law.
1768 Returned to Edinburgh. Became partner of George Inglis.
1769 *Virginia; or The Roman Father,* unpublished tragedy, completed.
1771 April, *The Man of Feeling* published. May, *The Pursuits of Happiness,* semisatirical poem, published.
1773 February, *The Man of the World,* novel, published. March 8, first performance of *The Prince of Tunis,* tragedy, in Edinburgh. Purchased Crown practice in Court of Exchequer from his partner, George Inglis.
1776 January 6, married Penuel Grant; has fourteen children.
1777 April, *Julia de Roubigné,* epistolary novel, published.
1779 January 23, *Mirror* began publication.
1780 May 27, *Mirror* ceased publication.
1784 February 10, *The Shipwreck,* adaptation of Lillo's *Fatal Curiosity;* one performance at Covent Garden.
1785 February 5, *Lounger* began publication.
1787 January 6, *Lounger* ceased publication.
1788 April 21, "Account of the German Theatre" read before the Royal Society of Edinburgh.
1789 December 5, *The Force of Fashion,* comedy; one performance at Covent Garden.

1790 April, *Letters of Brutus* began to be published in the *Edinburgh Herald.*

1791 *Letters of Brutus to Certain Celebrated Political Characters*, first series, published in collected form.

1792 Publication of *Review of the Principal Proceedings of the Parliament of 1784.*

1793 *Letters of Brutus*, second series, published in collected form. "Some Account of the Life and Writings of Dr. Blacklock" prefixed to a new edition of Blacklock's works.

1798 December 7, death of John Mackenzie, his youngest son, at age of six.

1799 Appointed Comptroller of Taxes for Scotland.

1800 February 18, death of Dr. Joshua Mackenzie, his father, at age of eighty-six.

1805 Publication of *Report of the Committee of the Highland Society of Scotland, appointed to inquire into the nature and authenticity of the poems of Ossian. Drawn up by Henry Mackenzie, Esq., its convener or chairman.*

1808 Authorized edition of *Works* published.

1814 Sir Walter Scott dedicated *Waverley* to Mackenzie, "Our Scottish Addison."

1822 *Account of the Life and Writings of John Home* published.

1824 Began to write his *Anecdotes and Egotisms*, reminiscences first published in 1927.

1831 Died on January 14. Buried in old Greyfriars Churchyard, Edinburgh.

CHAPTER 1

Mackenzie's Literary Career

I *Family Background*

ON August 6, 1745 (n.s.), the day Charles Edward, the Young Pretender, landed in Scotland, Henry Mackenzie was born into a prosperous and respected middle-class family in Edinburgh. His father, Dr. Joshua Mackenzie, after having served as a regimental surgeon in Ireland, had established a flourishing practice in Edinburgh and had married in August, 1744, Miss Margaret Rose of Kilravock, daughter of the sixteenth baron of Kilravock. While Dr. Mackenzie was directly descended from the eighth baron of Kintail, Chief of Clan Mackenzie, Henry's mother was related to many of the best families of Scotland. This pedigree later assured Mackenzie entrance into Edinburgh society.

Though Henry's mother died when he was only fourteen, her influence on her firstborn must have been profound. The Rose family "cultivated hospitality and kindness, music and letters, from one generation to another,"[1] and Margaret, whose favorite author was Mrs. Elizabeth Rowe, would likely have given direction and encouragement to her son's awakening literary interests. As a boy, Henry would accompany his mother to the fashionable tea tables of Edinburgh society, although, out of consideration for her friends, she would not allow her son's presence when a lady "who had no family or who had lost her children" visited her.[2] Such concern for others became ingrained in Mackenzie's character. In old age, he would observe with dismay the degeneration of manners: "Our young men care for nobody but themselves. You shall see them press to the fire on the coldest day, stand with their back to it, and pick their teeth, while ladies and old men are shivering at a distance."[3]

Mackenzie's principal link with the past was his maternal grandfather. Hugh Rose of Kilravock had been a member of Parliament and "a favourite of Sir Robert [Walpole]."[4] He "was one of the best shots in the north of Scotland,"[5] a talented violinist, and a born storyteller. As a young boy, Henry frequently lived at Kilravock Castle and listened to his grandfather's anecdotes about the Rebellion of '45 and the visit paid by Prince Charlie to the laird on the eve of the Battle of Culloden.[6] Such tales inspired the youth with that pride in his Highland ancestry and heritage which found later expression in Mackenzie's "Story of Albert Bane" (*Lounger*, No. 61) and in the support he gave to the establishment of the Highland Society of Scotland.

Henry's father, who lived to be eighty-six years old, shared Hugh Rose's love for music and the outdoor life. Dr. Mackenzie played the German flute and was an accomplished vocalist. His son later recalled: "My father was a remarkably good singer, and during some of our journeys used to hum some airs, his favorites, which now swell my bosom and almost draw tears from my eyes."[7] Mackenzie also admired his father's skill as an angler and himself became a lifelong sportsman. More important, Dr. Mackenzie passed on to his son his own amiable, good-humored disposition. Announcing to his father-in-law the birth of another child, Dr. Mackenzie reveals not only his geniality, but a liberal view of religion that Henry came to share: "As nothing can be more agreeable than to tell good news, I have the pleasure to acquaint you, that yesterday, about five in the morning (being Easter Monday), your daughter brought you another grandson. In the evening I got your friend Peter Cuming (who, though a clergyman, is a sensible and honest fellow) to make him a Christian, so far as form goes."[8]

II *Education*

Mackenzie attended Edinburgh High School from 1751 to 1757. Since the curriculum was heavily oriented toward the classical Latin writers, his reading of Livy may have included the story of Virginia and thus suggested to him the subject for what was to become his first tragedy. In any event, his interest in the theater was kindled in these years. A speech from Virgil at the annual examination "attracted much notice," Mackenzie recollected, "from the impassioned manner in which I spoke it, having early a turn for theatrical studies."[9] His real initiation into the theatrical world came about through Mr. Callender, the manager of the Edinburgh Theatre (1756–59), who obtained Dr. Mackenzie's reluctant consent to introduce the eager youth "into the arcana of the histrionic art behind the scenes."[10] This was the period during which John Home's *Douglas* triumphed on the Edinburgh stage, and Mackenzie later recalled:

> I was then [1756] a boy, but of an age to be sometimes admitted as a sort of page to the tea-drinking parties of Edinburgh. I have a perfect recollection of the strong sensation which Douglas excited among its inhabitants. The men talked of the rehearsals; the ladies repeated what they had heard of the story; some had procured, as a great favour, copies of the most striking passages, which they recited at the earnest request of the company. I was present at the representation; the applause was enthusiastic; but a better criterion of its merits was the tears of the audience, which the tender part of the drama drew forth unsparingly.[11]

That the "tears of the audience" demonstrate a play's "merits" was a lesson Mackenzie was never to forget. Underlying all his tragedies is the assumption that the playwright's main purpose is to evoke specific emotional responses from his audience.

Mackenzie attended Edinburgh University from 1758 to 1761, coming under the influence of Professor John Stevenson, whose lectures on literature had earlier inspired Hugh Blair and William Robertson. Equally important in Mackenzie's development were the literary and debating societies that flourished at Scottish universities. Here future clergymen, lawyers, and academicians argued over such subjects as "The Government of the Passions," "The Extent and Limits of Human Reason," and "The Pleasures of Virtue and Solitude."[12] Mackenzie's love of such societies continued into adulthood and resulted, some fifteen years later, in his participation in the Mirror Club and a new direction for his literary career—periodical essayist and editor.

III *The Young Poet*

That career had begun, inauspiciously enough, with a group of lyrical and descriptive poems published anonymously in the *Scots Magazine* between 1763 and 1765. Mackenzie was by now a law clerk, having been articled in 1761 for five years to Mr. George Inglis, King's Attorney in Exchequer. Buoyed up by the publication of his first poem, "Happiness," Mackenzie ventured to submit further verse to *Scots Magazine*: "I was delighted to find it ["Happiness"] in the next number of the magazine [November, 1763], and continued to send them pieces of poetry; but so shy was I of being known as their author, that I used to go to Sands's shop after it was dark and deliver the MSS. in silence to the shop-boy."[13]

As typical juvenilia, these poems are of little intrinsic worth, though they already reveal Mackenzie's idealism. In "Happiness," composed at the age of eighteen, he writes:

> As for my Fortune let a small Estate
> Dispose me rather to be good than great
> Enough to use it with an open Heart
> To serve my Wants & throw Distress a Part.[14]

Far superior are two heroic ballads also published during the same period in *Scots Magazine*: "Duncan" (1764), purported to be "from an old Scots manuscript," and "Kenneth, a Fragment" (1765), which Harold Thompson, Mackenzie's biographer, has called "the finest romantic ballad composed in Britain in the eighteenth century."[15]

Somewhat later, Mackenzie wrote "The Vision of Vanity," a didactic poem that seeks through a series of satirical portraits to demonstrate the vanity behind all human motivation. The poem is of some importance because it already shows that concern with sham forms of sensibility which later dominates many of Mackenzie's periodical essays. Daphne, one of the characters portrayed, is a writer of sentiment; and, though she insists on strict poetic justice in her novels, she "lost her virtue—while she wrote its praise." Although "The Vision of Vanity" was never published until it appeared in Mackenzie's collected *Works* (1808), it became, according to his own admission, a preliminary sketch for his most ambitious poem, *The Pursuits of Happiness,* finished in 1770, soon after the completion of *The Man of Feeling.* Again the theme is that "Instinctive vanity rules all mankind," but its development is more complex than that of "The Vision of Vanity." *The Pursuits of Happiness* contains obvious echoes from Alexander Pope's *Essay on Man*:

> Come, then, and let us lecture by the hour
> On these great subjects, Wisdom, Wealth, and Power,
> The boasted source of every bliss deny,
> And shew their empty urns, their fountains dry. (VIII, 68–69)[16]

But there is also Pope's modulation of tone that makes this poem far more effective than its predecessor, "The Vision of Vanity." Mackenzie can be indignant: "The blushless sons of these degenerate days, / Not virtue scorn alone, but virtue's praise." Or he can be sardonic in a manner reminiscent of Pope's *Moral Essays*:

> Thus honest Balaam—yes, the title's meet,
> No rich man is a rogue in Lombard-street—
> "What! honest? he, whom orphan minors curse,
> Robbed of their rights to pamper Balaam's purse;
> A suit in chancery shall set you right"—
> A knave! I scorn the word—the man's a knight . . . (VIII, 74–75)[17]

Or he can become pensive and personal:

> How would they view me from their crowds retire,
> To feast on thought beside my evening fire!
> By nature formed to dwell on fancy's themes,
> With sacred faith I hear her wildest dreams;
> On all her clouds impress a livelier glow,
> And flush the painting of her gaudiest bow. (VIII, 85)

Nevertheless, despite Mackenzie's increased skill, *The Pursuits of Happiness* was poorly received by reviewers on its publication in May, 1771,[18] and proved to be the author's last significant poem.

IV *The Novelist*

Mackenzie's literary aspirations had, in any case, already found a new direction: the abortive poet was on his way to becoming the leading British novelist of the 1770's. In November, 1765, Mackenzie had been admitted attorney in the Court of Exchequer of Scotland, though he was not yet of age, because of "a favourable opportunity of going to London and attending the Exchequer of England."[19] It was during this stay in the English capital (1765–68) that the young Scotsman conceived the outline for his first novel: "Of *The Man of Feeling* . . . the idea was first adopted in London whither I went for instruction in English law and English forms which by a particular sort of anomaly, directed by the Act of Union, were the law and practice of the Exchequer of Scotland."[20]

We know very little about this period in Mackenzie's life or why he began to plan a sentimental novel. The popularity of Oliver Goldsmith's *The Vicar of Wakefield* (1766), which Mackenzie admired and to which his novel shows affinities, may have spurred him on to try his hand at writing fiction. While the sentimental novel undoubtedly appealed to him temperamentally, its growing popularity must have impressed him as well. The success of such works as Jean Jacques Rousseau's *La Nouvelle Héloïse* (1761), Laurence Sterne's *Sentimental Journey* (1768), and Henry Brooke's *Fool of Quality* (1766–70) suggests, in fact, a highly receptive reading public that was eager to indulge its feelings and give proof of the strength of its sensibility. Since the philosophical background for this phenomenon and for Mackenzie's fiction is discussed later (particularly, in Chapters 2 and 3), it need not concern us here.

In the summer of 1768, his English legal studies completed, Mackenzie returned home although sorely tempted to remain and practice law in London: "I was strongly urged by an intimate friend of the legal profession who was well acquainted with barristers and attorneys, to remain in London and get myself called to the Bar there, . . . but the love of home and the desire of my family prevailed, and I returned to Edinburgh under the patronage of Mr. Inglis."[21] His former master not only welcomed him back, but soon made him his partner. By

November, 1768, the first reference to *The Man of Feeling* appears in Mackenzie's letters to his cousin, Elizabeth Rose of Kilravock: "Of all the Garbs I ever saw Pride put on, that of her Humility is to me the most disgusting. Pray did my Aunt Lexie mention any thing to you of a young Gentleman one Harley [hero of *The Man of Feeling*] with whom She & I were a little acquainted at Fowlis? this last was a Sentiment of his."[22]

Mackenzie's first novel was published in April, 1771, and by June he could boast to his cousin: "the Reception which the public Indulgence has given it has exceeded my Expectations: the copies allotted for Edin^r were all sold in about a Week's Time, & when a fresh Demand was made on London it was found that the whole Impression had been already exhausted."[23] Such was its popular success that *The Man of Feeling* quickly became a status symbol among fashionable women. To quote Henry Graham, "The libraries of Tunbridge Wells, Bath, and Cheltenham were besieged by ladies demanding to be the first to read it; it lay on the drawing-room tables of every one pretending to fashion, who, jaded with routs and gaming-tables, wept till their rouged and powdered cheeks presented runnels of tears, like cracks on old china, over 'dear, good Mr. Harley,' who would not let a beggar pass without a shilling and a sigh, though the reader herself would not cross a puddle to save a life."[24]

Mackenzie wasted little time in following up his success with a counterpart to his first novel, entitled *The Man of the World* and published in February, 1773. In the following month, *The Prince of Tunis*, a tragedy written "several years" earlier, opened at the Theatre Royal in Edinburgh for a six-night run; and by the end of 1773, Mackenzie succeeded his partner, George Inglis, as King's Attorney in the Court of Exchequer. Less time now remained for writing, particularly after his marriage on January 6, 1776, to Penuel Grant, daughter of Sir Ludovick Grant, Chief of Clan Grant. It was a happy union, it produced fourteen children, most of whom survived into adulthood, and it proved socially advantageous for Mackenzie since Miss Grant was the granddaughter of the Earl of Findlater and Seafield. By May, 1776, Mackenzie admits to his cousin: "I am now in a Situation of solid Business that does not allow of those

Excursions into the Regions of Fancy which I used to indulge myself with."[25] Nevertheless, he did complete one more novel, *Julia de Roubigné,* published in 1777, with an introduction that the author calls a "parting address" to his readers.

V *Editor of the* Mirror *and* Lounger

If his days as a novelist were over, Mackenzie's literary career was far from finished. Near the end of 1777, his close friend William Craig invited him to join the Mirror Club, a group of young Edinburgh lawyers who met to discuss "subjects of manners, of taste, and of literature." They soon began to "put their thoughts into writing"[26] and decided to publish some of the papers for the express purpose of investigating "those passions and affections of the mind which have the chief influence on the happiness of individuals, or of society."[27] Since no one except Mackenzie had ever published, he became the *Mirror*'s editor as well as its chief contributor. Between January 23, 1779, and May 27, 1780, one hundred ten numbers were published; and, though individual issues were poorly received, the collected three-volume set sold well, going through five editions by 1783. The same group of lawyers, with Mackenzie again taking the leading role, subsequently brought out the *Lounger,* issuing a hundred and one papers between February 5, 1785, and January 6, 1787.[28]

The papers that Mackenzie wrote, nearly forty for the *Mirror* and more than fifty for the *Lounger* (as well as parts of other essays), form a significant body of his work and reveal a versatility of style and interest that is rarely acknowledged. He can be lucid and informative, as in the two introductory essays of the *Lounger;* lightly sardonic, as in his essay on advertisement in *Mirror,* No. 80; or pensive, as when he recounts the death of a young girl in *Mirror,* No. 72. Aside from his tales and critical essays, which are discussed in Chapters 5 and 7, respectively, the most significant of these papers—eight in all— present an episodic narrative about the Homespun and Mushroom families that started in the *Mirror* and continued in the *Lounger.* The series begins with a letter from John Homespun (*Mirror,* No. 12), "a plain country-gentleman, with a small fortune," who complains that his two eldest unmarried daughters have had their taste and manners perverted as a result of a month's stay with a neighboring "great lady." Conditions grow worse in the next episode (*Mirror,* No. 25) when the lady pays the Homespun family a visit and succeeds in corrupting the rest of the household: "My gardner has tied his hair behind, and stolen my flour to powder it... I found a great hoyden, who washes my daughter's linens, sitting, the other afternoon, dressed in one of their cast fly-caps, entertaining this same oaf of a gardner, and the wives of two of my farm-servants, with tea, forsooth." The situation is partly resolved in *Mirror,* No. 53, written by Eliza Homespun, one of the daughters. Having been snubbed by Lady —— in Edinburgh, Eliza is forced to recognize her idol's shallowness and insincerity.

New complications arise, however, when the series is resumed in *Lounger,* No. 17. Though Eliza is now married to a "plain, virtuous, thriving young man," a "new plague" threatens John Homespun's family with the return of "neighbour Mushroom's son" from India with a fortune of a hundred thousand pounds. Behaving in true *nouveau riche* fashion, young Mushroom's wife becomes the envy of Homespun's wife and daughters. There follow three letters (*Lounger,* Nos. 36, 56, 62) by Marjorie Mushroom, the nabob's sister, to suggest that life at Mushroom-Hall is hardly as desirable as it may appear, for "it is so troublesome an affair to be fashionable." Yet, after visiting Edinburgh, she finds the country strangely changed and dreams longingly of fashionable life in town. In the last letter (*Lounger*, No. 98), John Homespun resumes his account and describes a dinner at the house of the "great lady," who had previously corrupted his family and who is now campaigning for young Mushroom's election to Parliament.

The whole series is an entertaining social picture and reveals Mackenzie's superb mastery of light comedy. "The historian of the Homespun family," Sir Walter Scott wrote, "may place his narrative, without fear of shame, by the side of *The Vicar of Wakefield.*"[29] Yet behind Mackenzie's amusing account lies a more serious purpose: like so many of his class, he feared that the sudden accumulation of wealth would lead not only to social upheaval but to a decline in morality and taste. "The Tribute paid to Grandeur or Wealth," he wrote to his cousin, "is ever in an inverse Proportion to the Virtue of a People. Commercial Nations like ours are peculiarly subject to it from the sudden Influx of Riches to which they are liable."[30] Such conservatism was probably the impetus also for Colonel Caustic, a character reminiscent of Sir Roger de Coverley, who appears in six of Mackenzie's *Lounger* papers and whom he describes as "a fine gentleman of the last age, somewhat severe in his remarks on the present."

VI *Man of Letters*

Mackenzie, by now one of the acknowledged leaders of Scotland's literati, helped to found the Royal Society of Edinburgh and also edited the early volumes of its *Transactions.* He played whist and piquet with an aging David Hume, became the close friend of Adam Ferguson and Dugald Stewart, and was frequently in the society of Adam Smith, William Robertson, and Hugh Blair. His novels had made Mackenzie a celebrity, and visitors to Edinburgh were accustomed to seek out "The Man of Feeling." As a young poet, Samuel Rogers visited the Scottish capital in 1789 and when asked by his host, Adam Smith, "whom he desired most to meet, . . . Rogers answered, 'The author of *Julia de Roubigné.*' "[31] Robert Burns went so far as to prize *The Man of Feeling* "next to the Bible,"[32] and upon Burns's death a writer in *Scots Magazine* pointed out that Mackenzie's novel had been "his *vade mecum*": "we have heard him say, that, by carrying it in his pocket, he wore out two copies of that elegant and bewitching novel."[33]

Mackenzie, perhaps more than anyone, had been instrumental in launching Burns's fame with *Lounger*, No. 97, "Extraordinary account of Robert Burns, the Ayrshire plowman; with extracts from his poems," published December 9, 1786. Like most of Edinburgh's literati, Mackenzie wished to see Scotland's new bard as a rustic and untutored genius, a misconception Burns himself obligingly fostered in his preface to the Kilmarnock volume.[34] "With what uncommon penetration and sagacity," Mackenzie exclaims, "this Heaven-taught plowman, from his humble and unlettered station, has looked upon men and manners." Both the *Scots Magazine* and *Edinburgh Magazine* reprinted *Lounger,* No. 97, and spread Burns's fame through Scotland and England, though Burns himself voiced misgivings about his new social position: "Dugald Stewart and some of my learned friends [Stewart introduced Mackenzie to Burns's poetry] put me in the periodical paper called The Lounger, a copy of which I here inclose you [John Ballantine].—I was, Sir, when I was first honored with your notice, too obscure, now I tremble lest I should be ruined by being dragged to [*sic*] suddenly into the glare of polite & learned observation."[35]

Equally influential was Mackenzie's "Account of the German Theatre," read before the Royal Society of Edinburgh in 1788 and published in 1790. Though he knew no German and had to depend upon two collections of French translations, his lecture, nevertheless, did much to introduce German literature to the English reader. Most important is Mackenzie's acclaim of Friedrich von Schiller and his first play, *Die Räuber,* to which the last fourth of the paper is devoted. He views Schiller, like Burns, as an original genius, who, although he ignores "dramatic regularity," has yet created "characters and situations of the most interesting and impressive kind, and has endowed those characters with a language in the highest degree eloquent, impassioned and sublime."[36]

Mackenzie's paper aroused young Walter Scott's interest in German poetry, leading not only to Scott's study of the language, but to the translating of two ballads by Gottfried August Bürger in 1796 and hence the beginning of Scott's poetic career.[37] Some eighteen years later, Mackenzie also helped to launch Scott as a novelist. A cautious James Ballantyne, Scott's publisher, hesitant about printing a thousand copies of *Waverley,* entrusted the opening chapters to Mackenzie for his opinion. Unaware of the author's identity, Mackenzie wasted no time in reassuring Ballantyne. Robert Pierce Gillies, a contemporary observer of the literary scene, recalls "with what fervent zeal the patriarchial critic [Mackenzie] hurried and drifted along the streets at his fleetest pace, to express his conviction that this would turn out to be no ordinary novel, and, whatever the publisher might think, it was 'not the work of any ordinary man.' "[38]

In 1790, as events in France were approaching their violent climax, Mackenzie assumed a new role as a political writer and later as a propagandist for William Pitt's Tory government. His *Letters of Brutus to Certain Celebrated Political Characters*, published originally in two series in the *Edinburgh Herald* (1790–92), were primarily aimed at the three great Whig orators: Richard Brinsley Sheridan, Edmund Burke, and Charles James Fox. Though the letters are of relatively little literary interest, they reveal again Mackenzie's considerable satirical power. With devastating sarcasm, he addresses General Burgoyne, who was defeated at the battle of Saratoga (1777): "It has been your peculiar ill fortune, Sir, to meet with distressful and mortifying circumstances, which neither improved your mind, nor produced compassion for its weakness. Your own estimation of your abilities always kept pace with the proofs of your incapacity; and you claimed from the world its respect and applause, in moments when you should have left it to forget its contempt, or to retain its indifference."[39]

VII "Revenant *from another epoch*"

Though Mackenzie was only forty-five years old in 1790, his major creative period had virtually ended in 1789 with his only comedy, *The Force of Fashion*, preceded five years earlier by *The Shipwreck*, an adaptation of Lillo's *Fatal Curiosity*. Henceforth, his principal writing was biographical, culminating in his *Account of the Life and Writings of John Home* in 1822. It is difficult to account for such a creative decline. No doubt, his professional duties, particularly after he was made Comptroller of Taxes for Scotland in 1799, left him little leisure. Nevertheless, other factors affected Mackenzie's creativity. In 1802, writing to Dr. James Currie, the biographer of Burns, he contended: "notwithstanding the partial Opinion of my Friends, want of Ability as well as of Inclination disqualify me for resuming my Pen. Feelings of severe Affliction, repressed & therefore the less overcome, have broken down, somewhat before their time, my Mind as well as Body."[40] Mackenzie may in part be referring to the death of his youngest son, John, who died at the age of six on December 7, 1798. In a moving letter to

William Craig, written the following morning, he revealed the depth of his feelings:

> I am now easier but have had a terrible night. All day I had kept myself up to perform those little offices & forms which the situation required. I had put this seal of constraint on my heart but when night & solitude came, it burst out with double force, & had effects more violent than any I had ever felt, or could have supposed myself subject to. Through the day I was a sort of third person, the night restored me to myself & to the full consciousness of my affliction. You will perhaps wonder at those feelings being so strongly exerted at the loss of a child of 6 years old—
>
> I doted perhaps too much on him, & he was particularly fond of me. Of late he was the favourite companion, & his innocent prattle the amusement of my country walks.[41]

While it is difficut to measure the overall effect of this experience on Mackenzie, there is an increasing note of bitterness if not disillusionment in his writings that is epitomized by some lines jotted down in 1805: "At *twenty*, I read Rochefoucauld with indignation; at *forty*, with Doubt;—now at *Sixty*, almost, tho' unwillingly, with Conviction of the truth of his Maxims."[42]

Mackenzie was to live another twenty-five years, surviving all of his contemporary friends to become the last link with the era of Hume and Adam Smith, and the grand old man of Scottish letters. R. P. Gillies has left us a description of the aged Mackenzie taking his habitual walk through the streets of Edinburgh:

> No weather daunted him. During squalls, not uncommon at Edinburgh, such as I would not willingly have encountered, I have observed him both early and late (often attended by a favourite pointer) drifting along with the tempest, or tottering beneath its attacks, yet by inflexible resolution bidding defiance to both wind and rain. Considering his advanced age, his attenuated form, wrapped in a long, dark surtout, which always seemed too wide, as if only a skeleton were under it, and his countenance, then worn and sharpened, like that of Voltaire in his very last days, and yet capable at all times of the most animated expression, he appeared to me in the same light as Goethe afterwards did in the year 1822; that is to say, he was like a *revenant* from another epoch, at which time *our* world was not in being.[43]

On January 17, 1831, Sir Walter Scott noted in his diary: "I got notice of poor Henry Mackenzie's death [he died on January 14]. He has long maintained a niche in Scottish literature—gayest of the gay, though most sensitive of the sentimental."[44]

CHAPTER 2

The Man of Feeling

THE *Man of Feeling,* Mackenzie's first novel, was written between 1768 and 1770 and published the following year. Its main action can quickly be summarized. Harley, an orphan since childhood, is left with "a variety of guardians," whose perpetual disagreements leave his education "indifferently attended to." When Harley is advised to increase his meager estate by seeking "a lease of some crown-lands" adjacent to his property, he sets off for London after taking leave of his maiden aunt and his neighbor's daughter, Miss Walton, whom he secretly loves. He attempts to gain a baronet's favor in his behalf and comes in contact with the corruption of London: he mistakes a former footman and pimp for a gentleman, is fleeced by a group of sharpers, and takes a Bedlam inmate to be a guide. He weeps over the plaintive story of a mad girl, and he listens attentively to the diatribe of a disillusioned misanthrope.

Thus far, Harley has been largely a passive observer; however, his reaction to the plight of a starving prostitute rouses him into action. He feeds Emily Atkins, gives her his last half-guinea, and succeeds in reconciling her to her father. Then, having failed to obtain the lease, he journeys home. On the stagecoach, he bravely reproves an impudent officer and discusses "poetical inclination" with an old gentleman. Nearing home, he meets old Edwards returning from military service in India, where he had gone to keep his son from the clutches of a press gang. They arrive home only to find Edwards's son and daughter-in-law dead of "broken hearts." Harley bestows a small farm on Edwards and his grandchildren and learns of Miss Walton's impending marriage to Sir Harry Benson. The news proves to be false, but Harley's health declines after he catches a fever in attending the ailing Edwards. Believing himself to be dying, he finally admits his love to Miss Walton; and, upon her returning his affections, Harley expires contented.

I *Harley's Ideal Character*

Though Mackenzie hoped that the reputation of his first novel "was of that reasonable kind which does not cease with the Breath that gave it,"[1] *The Man of Feeling* is today, according to David Daiches, "largely a historical curiosity."[2] It has become one of the traditional works to cite in describing the eighteenth-century sentimental novel, for its hero has become the example *par excellence* of the effete and mawkish Man of Feeling. Inevitably, such categorizing oversimplifies and distorts Harley's character. Literary historians, who never tire of ascribing his death entirely to excessive sensibility,[3] conveniently ignore the fact that Harley had imperfectly recovered from "a very dangerous fever" and that "his health was manifestly on the decline" (I, 231).

This is not to deny Harley's intense sensibility but to see it in its proper perspective. For Mackenzie, sensibility can become a beneficial and moral quality, though it can also be perverted for egotistical ends. To understand his concept, it is useful to turn to the philosophical writings of Adam Smith. Mackenzie was intimately acquainted with Smith, particularly after Smith began to reside in Edinburgh in 1778.[4] In a letter to William Carmichael, American Chargé d'Affaires in Spain, Mackenzie observed: "*Dr. Smith,* whom I reckon the first of our Writers, both in point of Genius & Information, is now revising both his Theory of Moral Sentiments, & his Essay on the Wealth of Nations, in the new Editions of both which (to be published in the Spring) there will be considerable alteration & Improvements."[5] That Mackenzie had read *The Theory of Moral Sentiments* (1759) is fairly evident from the reference he makes to it in an unpublished philosophical essay: "This division [between improper and unjust vices] is noticed and most ingeniously explained by the celebrated Adam Smith in his theory of moral Sentiments. We observe that our moral disapprobation of acts of impropriety does not arise so much from any perception of the evil that springs from them as from a direct want of sympathy with the agent."[6] Smith's treatise had, in effect, a profound influence upon Mackenzie's literary works because it provided him with a comprehensive theory of individual psychology.

At the outset of his *Theory*, Smith assumes, as David Hume had before him, that men have a natural propensity, though in different degrees, to commiserate with the suffering of their fellow beings. Such sympathy results not from directly perceiving the sufferer's feelings but from empathy: "As we have no immediate experience of what other men feel, we can form no idea of the manner in which they are affected, but by conceiving what we ourselves should feel in the like situation."[7] Since sympathy thus depends upon our own impressions, those who possess the keenest sensitivity tend to be most responsive and likely most compassionate, even to extremes. Sympathy comes, therefore, to be associated with a highly refined sensibility: "The amiable virtue of humanity requires, surely, a sensibility, much beyond what is possessed by the rude vulgar of mankind."[8] Such an assumption, as we will see, often had the unfortunate result of turning sensibility into a status symbol in the latter decades of the century.

Empathy depends, however, not only on one's emotional susceptibility but upon the power of one's imagination:

> Though our brother is upon the rack, as long as we ourselves are at our ease, our senses will never inform us of what he suffers. They never did and never can carry us beyond our own person, and it is by the *imagination* only that we can form any conception of what are his sensations. Neither can that faculty help us to this any other way, than by representing to us what would be our own, if we were in his case. It is the impressions of our senses only, not those of his, which our *imaginations* copy [italics mine].[9]

A man's capacity for commiseration depends, therefore, upon both sensibility and imagination. As James Beattie points out: "Of sympathy all men are not equally susceptible. They who have a lively imagination, keen feelings, and what we call a tender heart, are most subject to it."[10]

Within such a context, the broad outline of Mackenzie's hero takes on a meaningful pattern. Harley's sensibility is characterized by his impulsiveness, a nervous kind of excitability that makes him respond almost instantly to an emotional experience. When he sees the schoolhouse of his childhood in ruins, he is overcome with grief and nostalgia: "'Oh heavens!' he cried, 'what do I see! silent, unroofed and desolate! Are all the gay tenants gone? Do I hear their hum no more? Edwards, look there, look there! the scene of my infant joys, my earliest friendships, laid waste and ruinous!'" (I, 176). He curses the squire who pulled it down because it obstructed his view; and, when he is taken to speak to the schoolmistress, "he followed her, without knowing whither he went." Harley can take an instant liking to a man if his face bespeaks honesty or denotes suffering. An old and crippled soldier asleep amidst a picturesque setting of nature ("which Salvator would have drawn") brings forth his "romantic enthusiasm" (I, 158), and his intense and vivacious affections know no moderation once they have been aroused (I, 26).

Along with such sensibility, Harley shows signs of a highly developed imagination. He traces portraits in the fire and is so moved by the pathos of Edwards's story that he "started with a convulsive sort of motion, and, grasping Edwards's sword, drew it half out of the scabbard, with a look of the most frantic wildness" (I, 168). Doubts about the wisdom of helping a prostitute vanish before "the warmth of his nature.... he recalled the languid form of the fainting wretch to his mind; he wept at the recollection of her tears" (I, 97). To quote Adam Smith, "it is by changing places in fancy with the sufferer, that we come either to conceive or to be affected by what he feels."[11]

Having an acute capacity to feel deeply and to put himself in another's place gives Harley a remarkable sympathy for his fellow men. He can imagine and feel their misery and, at the same time, be uneasily conscious of his own well-being. When he learns that the prostitute, Emily Atkins, has been starving for two days, "he fixed his eyes on her's—every circumstance but the last was forgotten; and he took her hand with as much respect as if she had been a duchess.... 'Two days!'—said he; 'and I have fared sumptuously every day!'" (I, 90).

To feel such compassion, however, requires little effort or sacrifice—it is merely an emotional response, what Smith defines as humanity to distinguish it from the higher virtue of generosity: "Humanity consists merely in the exquisite fellow-feeling which the spectator entertains with the sentiments of the persons principally concerned, so as to grieve for their sufferings, to resent their injuries, and to rejoice at their good fortune. The most humane actions require no self-denial, no self-command, no great exertion of the sense of propriety. They consist only in doing what this exquisite sympathy would of its own accord prompt us to do."[12] The virtue of humanity is best exemplified by Miss Walton, whose "beneficence was unbounded; indeed the natural tenderness of her heart might have been argued, by the frigidity of a casuist, as detracting from her virtue in this respect; for her humanity was a feeling, not a principle" (I, 24).[13]

Harley, however, is capable of sacrificing his own interest for the good of another. He cheerfully receives the news that the lease he has sought has been given to one "who had long served his majesty." Though the report proves false, this does not diminish the merit of his response: "Perhaps . . . some war-worn officer, who, like poor Atkins, had been neglected from reasons which merited the highest advancement; whose honour could not stoop to solicit the preferment he deserved; perhaps, with a family, taught the principles of delicacy, without the means of supporting it; a wife and children—gracious heaven! whom my wishes would have deprived of bread!" (I, 136–37). On another occasion, Harley risks his own life in order to nurse Edwards when the old man is stricken with a contagious disease; he thus catches the fever that later contributes to his death.

Such actions are truly generous because, as Smith points out,

> we prefer some other person to ourselves, and sacrifice some great and important interest of our own to an equal interest of a friend or of a superior. The man who gives up his pretensions to an office that was the great object of his ambition, because he imagines that the services of another are better entitled to it; the man who exposes his life to defend that of his friend, which he judges to be of more im-

portance, neither of them act from humanity, or because they feel more exquisitely what concerns that other person than what concerns themselves. They both consider those opposite interests not in the light in which they naturally appear to themselves, but in that in which they appear to others. To every bystander, the success or preservation of this other person may justly be more interesting than their own; but it cannot be so to themselves. When to the interest of this other person, therefore, they sacrifice their own, they accommodate themselves to the sentiments of the spectator, and by an effort of magnanimity act according to those views of things which they feel, must naturally occur to any third person.[14]

In essence, this "impartial spectator," or "man within," forms the apex of Smith's moral hierarchy built upon man's inherent sympathy, though the term for Smith denotes not merely pity or compassion but "fellow-feeling with any passion whatever."[15] Whereas compassion consists of "changing places in fancy with the sufferer," moral judgment depends upon putting oneself in the place of the agent as well as the recipient of the deed and determining how far one approves or disapproves their respective feelings. To Smith, a sense of merit arises then from "direct sympathy with the sentiments of the agents, and an indirect sympathy with the gratitude of those who receive the benefit of his actions." A sense of demerit stems conversely from "a direct antipathy to the sentiments of the agent, and an indirect sympathy with the resentment of the sufferer."[16] Now if we judge the conduct of others by putting ourselves in their situation, we judge our own actions with a similar kind of sympathy. Becoming critical of other people's conduct naturally leads us to wonder how our behavior appears to them:

We begin, upon this account to examine our own passions and conduct, and to consider how these must appear to them, by considering how they would appear to us if in their situation. We suppose ourselves the spectators of our own behaviour, and endeavour to imagine what effect it would, in this light, produce upon us. This is the only looking-glass by which we can, in some measure, with the eyes of others, scrutinize the propriety of our own conduct. If in this view it pleases us, we are tolerably satisfied. We can be more indifferent about the applause, and, in some measure, despise the censure of others; secure that, however misunderstood or misrepresented, we are the natural and proper objects of approbation.[17]

Through the development and refinement of the "impartial spectator," man is able to rise above the often unreliable judgment of his fellow men—the "man without." Such an inner-directed person, to use a modern term, does not heed men's praise of his actions unless he finds them praiseworthy, nor their blame unless he himself condemns them.

Yet few, if any, can consistently preserve such a degree of moral perfection. According to Smith, man is too prone to view his own conduct subjectively; he is blinded by self-interest and is reluctant to "pull off the mysterious veil of self-delusion."[18] Nor is even the "man within" immune from such aberrations: "Even in good men, the judge within is often in danger of being corrupted by the violence and injustice of their selfish passions, and is often induced to make a report very different from what the real circumstances of the case are capable of authorizing."[19] As a corrective to such a failing, man falls back upon the guidance of those "general rules of conduct" that each has formed for himself from observing human behavior and from noting his own reaction to the conduct of others:

None but those of the happiest mould are capable of suiting, with exact justness, their sentiments and behaviour to the smallest difference of situation, and of acting upon all occasions with the most delicate and accurate propriety. The coarse clay of which the bulk of mankind are formed, cannot be wrought up to such perfection. There is scarce any man, however, who by discipline, education, and example, may not be so impressed with a regard to general rules, as to act upon almost every occasion with tolerable decency, and through the whole of his life avoid any considerable degree of blame.[20]

Harley, it seems clear, possesses this ideal justness of behavior. We are told that in him "the most delicate consciousness of propriety often kindled that blush which marred the performance of it" (I, 26). Governed by the "man within," confident in his own values, he rejects the world's standard of conduct though he earns thereby its mockery and contempt.

"The world is ever tyrannical," he tells Captain Atkins; "it warps our sorrows to edge them with keener affliction: let us not be slaves to the names it affixes to motive or to action. I know an ingenuous mind cannot help feeling when they sting: but there are considerations by which it may be overcome: its fantastic ideas vanish as they rise; they teach us—to look beyond it" (I, 134–35). Yet Harley is too self-conscious to remain totally indifferent to the censure of the "man without." Indeed, his habitual bashfulness symbolizes this underlying tension: "I was not formed for the bustle of the busy, nor the dissipation of the gay; a thousand things occurred, where I blushed for the impropriety of my conduct when I thought on the world, though my reason told me I should have blushed to have done otherwise. It was a scene of dissimulation, of restraint, of disappointment" (I, 233–34).

II *Tone*

Not surprisingly, Harley chooses "to live sequestered from the noise of the multitude." "The world," he complains, "is in general selfish, interested, and unthinking, and throws the imputation of romance, or melancholy, on every temper more susceptible than its own" (I, 235). This conflict between the idealistic, highly sensitive individual and a materialistic, callous society becomes Mackenzie's central subject. As a theme, it was hardly original in eighteenth-century fiction—we are particularly reminded of Sarah Fielding's *David Simple* (1744), whose hero Harley somewhat resembles. Nor are the situations that befall him particularly novel.[21] What does distinguish *The Man of Feeling* is a singular and sustained tone of pathos, softened frequently by light comic touches. Though we admire Harley for his goodness and innocence, we also regret and pity his unfitness for life. At times, we smile at his excessive sensibility and humanity; but ours is an indulgent kind of humor, free of either ridicule or contempt. Mackenzie developed such an ambivalent tone by means of a sympathetic, though somewhat ironic, narrator.

The story opens with an account of how the history of Harley was supposedly discovered. While hunting "on a burning first of September," the narrator, who calls himself the book's editor, comes upon "a venerable pile" which his companion, the village curate, informs him was once the residence of Harley, "a whimsical sort of man." The curate carries with him a history of Harley, which he has found unreadable because it contains not a single syllogism and he can "never find the author in one strain for two chapters together." The manuscript was left behind by "a grave, oddish kind of a man, [who] boarded at a farmer's in this parish. The country people called him the ghost; and he was known by the slouch in his gait, and the length of his stride" (I, 4–5). The "ghost" (later called Charles) is an outsider who prefers the company of children to that of the villagers, for which the prosaic clergyman has labeled him "oddish" just as he has characterized Harley as "whimsical." The curate, perhaps representative of a callous society,[22] foreshadows its contempt and rejection of the Man of Feeling when he mutilates Charles's manuscript by using it as wadding for his rifle.

The editor, having perused the remaining pages, describes it apologetically as "a bundle of little episodes, put together without art, and of no importance on the whole; with something of nature, and little else in them." Yet he admits:

> I was a good deal affected with some very trifling passages in it; and had the name of a Marmontel, or a Richardson, been on the title-page,—'tis odds that I should have wept: But
>
> One is ashamed to be pleased with the works of one knows not whom. (I, 6)

The editor does not trust his own emotional response for fear of making himself look foolish. He needs the reassurance of social acceptance to believe in the testimony of his own feelings.

Mackenzie's introduction is more than the conventional claim of an eighteenth-century novelist for the authenticity of his work. By means of negative emphasis, he arouses the reader's sympathy for his central narrator before he makes his appearance. Hence our attitude toward Harley, in turn, becomes conditioned by Charles's account, and his sympathetic response becomes our own. To Charles, who has known and admired Harley, a visit to his grave is "worth a thousand homilies; every noble feeling rises within me! every beat of my heart awakens a virtue!—but it will make you hate the world—No: there is such an air of gentleness around, that I can hate nothing; but, as to the world—I pity the men of it" (I, 244). The narrator shares Harley's sensibility, but for him it has been qualified by a certain pessimism if not cynicism. A disillusioned idealist, Charles, like Goldsmith's Sir William Thornhill, prefers, as we have said, the company of children. Particularly qualified to be Harley's biographer, the narrator can understand and appreciate his subject's temperament yet view his excesses with some comic detachment. From such a perspective, his story is to be fashioned: "For some indeed a slender memorial will serve; and the soft affections, when they are busy that way, will build their structures, were it but on the paring of a nail" (I, 243).

At times the narrator serves as a chorus, berating an insensitive as well as insincere world, whose false values form an implicit antithesis to Harley's ideals and a source of tension for the novel: "Fashion, Bon ton, and Vertù, are the names of certain idols, to which we sacrifice the genuine pleasures of the soul: in this world of semblance, we are contented with personating happiness; to feel it, is an art beyond us" (I, 184). More often, however, the narrator's criticism is voiced ironically. When Harley's "worldly" guardians advise him to ingratiate himself with a rich relation, Charles relates that

> their hopes were disappointed; for the young man was so untoward in his disposition, that, notwithstanding the instructions he daily received, his visits rather tended to alienate than gain the good-will of his kinswoman. He sometimes looked grave when the old lady told the jokes of her youth; he often refused to eat when she pressed him, and was seldom or never provided with sugar-candy or liquorice when she was seized with a fit of coughing; nay, he had once the rudeness to fall asleep, while she was describing the composition and virtues of her favourite cholic-water. In short, he accommodated himself so ill to her humour, that she died, and did not leave him a farthing. (I, 17–18)

By pretending to describe the event from the point of view of the guardians, Charles ironically mocks their materialism and opportunism. Harley's "untoward" disposition, far from being a blemish, raises our respect for his integrity; though his behavior is also made comical by being presented through a mock-narrator: we can imagine the guardians' frustration and enjoy it because we condemn their values.

In other instances, however, Harley's actions evoke a less positive response. When he falls in love with Miss Walton, the narrator's tone shows more amused indulgence than admiration:

> It would be trite to observe the easy gradation from esteem to love: in the bosom of Harley there scarce needed a transition; for there were certain seasons when his ideas were flushed to a degree much above their common complexion. In times not credulous of inspiration, we should account for this from some natural cause; but we do not mean to account for it at all; it were sufficient to describe its effects; but they were sometimes so ludicrous, as might derogate from the dignity of the sensations which produced them to describe. They were treated indeed as such by most of Harley's sober friends, who often laughed very heartily at the awkward blunders of the real Harley, when the different faculties, which should have prevented them, were entirely occupied by the ideal. (I, 26–27)

The dominant note is a sense of the comic, if we use Meredith's definition of "being able to detect the ridicule of them you love without loving them less," for Charles's recognition of the "ludicrous" in Harley's behavior does not affect his love for his subject. Hence our response is the "laughter of comedy": "impersonal and of unrivaled politeness, nearer a smile—often no more than a smile."[23] The last sentence of the passage quoted above tends, moreover, to enhance our tolerance. The reaction of Harley's "sober friends" alludes to that "world of semblance" which has already been ironically derided; consequently, while we can smile over his "awkward blunders," we still prefer them to his friends' sobriety.

By such means, Mackenzie creates that soft ambivalent tone which pervades the novel. He succeeds in preserving the reader's sympathy and admiration for his hero in spite of the intellectual distance his narrator places between them.[24] Trying to account for Harley's naïveté, the narrator observes: "The optics of some minds are so unhappily constructed, as to throw a certain shade on every picture that is presented to them; while those of others (of which number was Harley,) like the mirrors of the ladies, have a wonderful effect in bettering their complexions" (I, 41–42). Harley's innocence evokes our respect rather than our contempt because we associate it with his idealism and benevolence. He is the characteristic *ingénu* whose naïveté, like the child's in "The Emperor's New Clothes," serves as an implicit critique of a corrupt society. Adam Smith describes such a temperament in terms that anticipate Harley's character and may well have influenced Mackenzie:

> There is a helplessness in the character of extreme humanity which more than any thing interests our pity. There is nothing in itself which renders it either ungraceful or disagreeable. We only regret that it is unfit for the world, because the world is unworthy of it, and because it must expose the person who is endowed with it as a prey to the perfidy and ingratitude of insinuating falsehood, and to a thousand pains and uneasinesses, which, of all men, he the least deserves to feel, and which generally too he is, of all men, the least capable of supporting.[25]

Harley's doubts about the honesty of the prostitute last for only a moment because "the torpor of such considerations was seldom prevalent over the warmth of his nature." When he resolves to meet her again, he exclaims that to "calculate the chances of deception is too tedious a business for the life of man" (I, 97–98). As a result of this attitude, he is frequently victimized by a rapacious and dissembling society. Not only is he deceived in such a world of appearances, but he also is misjudged in turn. Captain Atkins takes him for his daughter's seducer, and his London acquaintances assume from his own accounts that his corruption is near complete: "here's a very pretty fellow for you: to have heard him talk some nights ago, as I did, you might have sworn he was a saint; yet now he games with sharpers, and loses his money; and is bubbled by a fine story invented by a whore, and pawns his watch; here are sanctified doings with a witness!" (I, 96).

The truth is that Harley does resemble a saint, though Mackenzie undercuts such an impression with touches of the absurd and the mundane. We have already noted the comic tone with which Harley's love for Miss Walton is described, but more significant is the basis for that attachment. Because Harley is extremely bashful, Miss Walton pays more attention to him than to other guests in order "to bring to the line of that equality, which is ever necessary for the ease of our guests, those whose sensibility had placed them below it." Instead of Harley's falling in love with Miss Walton's goodness, as we would expect from such an incurable idealist, he responds to the flattery of his ego; for "notwithstanding the laboured definitions which very wise men have given us of the inherent beauty of virtue, we are always inclined to think her handsomest when she condescends to smile upon ourselves" (I, 25–26). Similarly, Mackenzie undercuts Harley's jealousy with humorous aspects of his distress: at the news of Miss Walton's supposedly impending marriage, he walks downstairs with one shoe unbuckled, the buckle in his hand; the pastoral that he composes to commemorate his distress he leaves behind "on the handle of a tea-kettle, at a neighbouring house."

Regardless of such foibles, however, Harley remains an idealized characterization. Steadily adhering to his own principles, refusing to compromise with an egotistical world, he represents for Mackenzie a highly attractive way of life. In part, the Man of Feeling is a self-portrait, partaking of his author's own experiences: "some of the incidents," Mackenzie later wrote, "I had a certain degree of share in myself. I was often the martyr of that shyness which Harley is stated as being affected by in his intercourse with mankind, and I had likewise the disgust at some parts of the legal profession to which I was destined."[26] The difference stems from the fact that Harley has no inclination for the law and refuses to heed the advice of one of his guardians while Mackenzie, with a similar aversion, yielded to practical considerations by becoming at the age of sixteen a clerk to Mr. George Inglis, King's Attorney in Exchequer.

In the character of the "brother of the misanthrope," Mackenzie depicted his own feelings at becoming indentured to a tax lawyer. ("That character and his disgust with his profession nearly my own case.")[27] We are told in *The Man of Feeling* that the younger brother

> was put apprentice to an eminent attorney. In this the expectations of his friends were more consulted than his own inclination; for . . . he had feelings of that warm kind, that could ill brook a study so dry as the law, especially in that department of it which was allotted to him. . . . The younger, from the gentleness of his nature, bore, with patience, a situation entirely discordant to his genius and disposition. At times, indeed, his pride would suggest, of how little importance those talents were, which the partiality of his friends had often extolled: they were now incumbrances in a walk of life where the dull and the ignorant passed him at every turn; his fancy and his feeling were invincible obstacles to eminence, in a situation, where his fancy had no room for exertion, and his feelings experienced perpetual disgust. (I, 63–64)

In *The Pursuits of Happiness*, published a month after *The Man of Feeling*, Mackenzie describes his own dilemma in a similar vein:

> Placed where no spark of genius dares to rise,
> Where dullness scarce unfolds her leaden eyes,
> With all th' inextricable maze around,
> Of Gothic jargon, and unmeaning sound . . . (VIII, 89)[28]

Mackenzie, it seems evident, recognized that he had compromised his own youthful ideals by choosing a profession that stifled his talents and his literary ambitions. Harley represents for him the ideal self, unfettered by worldly or selfish considerations and free to follow and perfect his own moral nature. But, while Mackenzie could admire and even envy such a figure, he was at the same time enough of a pragmatist[29] to recognize its unfitness for life.[30] From such conflicting feelings arises the ambivalent tone of the novel: he could love his hero and share his opinions of the world,[31] but he was not, like Harley, prepared to reject its allurement altogether. He could revere his hero's sensibility, pity his excessive humanity in an unfeeling world, but also sense a comic element in his quixotic nature. In the character of the idealistic yet somewhat disillusioned storyteller Charles, alienated from society and sympathetic to its victims, Mackenzie found the appropriate narrative perspective from which to view and delineate his hero.

III *Didacticism*

Though Harley's conflict with a corrupt society forms, as we have said, Mackenzie's major theme, it would be misleading to view his novel in the traditional terms of plot and structure. Dale Kramer suggests that we are shown Harley's gradual disillusionment upon "seeing the corrupted moral state of society and impossibility of distinguishing trustworthy virtue."[32] Yet, while it is true that a note of increasing bitterness is discernible in the second half of the novel, no clear pattern of causality and psychological change emerges. Mackenzie's purpose is more pictorial than dramatic: he aims to unfold Harley's portrait rather than to present his hero's education and disillusionment. Describing his novel to James Elphinston, he writes in a letter printed according to Elphinston's orthography: "It consists ov som eppisoddical adventures ov a *Man ov Feeling*: hware hiz sentiments ar occazzionally exprest, and dhe fetures ov hiz mind devellopt, az dhe incidents draw dhem foarth."[33]

We must not ignore the fragmented structure of the novel: to pretend that only twenty-two chapters, including three so-called fragments, remain out of the original fifty-six is not a mere whimsy or attempt to imitate Laurence Sterne. Rather it indicates a conscious effort to subordinate, at times even to disregard, causality and narrative sequence.[34] When Mackenzie sent his cousin the opening section of *The Man of Feeling,* he tried to provide some explanation for "a very whimsical introduction to a very odd medley":

> You must know then, that I have seldom been in Use to write any Prose, except what consisted of Observations (such as I could make) on Men & Manners. The way of introducing these by Narrative I had

fallen into in some detach'd Essays, from the Notion of it's interesting both the Memory & the Affection deeper, than mere Argument, or moral Reasoning. In this way I was somehow led to think of introducing a Man of Sensibility into different Scenes where his Feelings might be seen in their Effects, & his Sentiments occasionally delivered without the Stiffness of regular Deduction. In order to give myself entire Liberty in the Historical Part of the Performance, & to indulge that desultory Humour of writing which sometimes possesses me, I began with this Introduction & write now & then a Chapter as I have Leisure or Inclination.[35]

The desire to introduce such "Observations . . . on Men & Manners" into his novel was undoubtedly one of the motives for the loose, even desultory form that emerges. Some of these "detach'd Essays" are found in his "Passe-Temps," a notebook of largely unpublished poetry and prose, composed from 1763 to 1766. In these entries, a general observation is followed by an illustration in the form of a rudimentary tale, reminiscent of the form that eighteenth-century periodical essayists had perfected and one that Mackenzie himself used in his *Mirror* and *Lounger* essays. One such aphorism, composed by him at the age of nineteen, states that "the means of Happiness are often whimsical & far from being affixed to the Gifts of Fortune." A short exemplum follows about rich Varro who envies his poor neighbor Claudius for possessing an excellent dog, an ancient punch bowl, and a finely wrought snuffbox.[36]

In the novel, a stage-coach ride during which Harley meets Ben Silton becomes an opportunity for an extensive "narrative essay" about poetic inspiration (I, 148–51)—part of it, in fact, takes the form of an exemplum about two brothers that closely resembles the essays of his notebook. That such a discussion reflects Mackenzie's own views is demonstrated by the fact that excerpts from it frequently appear unacknowledged in his own letters[37] and that a brief part of Harley's remarks is derived from his notebook itself.[38] The pleasure of being benevolent, another topic Mackenzie injects into his novel (I, 80–81), although voiced by a swindler who is intent on fleecing Harley, is taken almost verbatim from another notebook essay.[39]

The latter two "fragments" of the novel were probably also originally "narrative essays," which Mackenzie found difficult to integrate into the main story. In the first of these, entitled ironically "The Man of Feeling talks of what he does not understand," Harley denounces the British conquest of India because it is motivated only by greed and has enriched the conquerors at the expense of the natives. Logically, Harley's "sentiments" should have been expressed when old Edwards had reached the point of his story where the old Indian is tortured to make him tell the location of his treasure. But, perhaps because such a digression would have undermined the pathos Mackenzie was developing through Edwards's tale, he placed it three chapters later. Edwards's new didactic role, however, makes his character inconsistent: he responds to Harley's attack by insisting that "there are great temptations in a great degree of riches, which it is no easy matter to resist: those a poor man like me cannot describe, because he never knew them; and perhaps I have reason to bless God that I never did; for then, it is likely, I should have withstood them no better than my neighbours" (I, 192). Mackenzie's purpose is to mitigate the severity of Harley's censure, but it is hardly plausible for Edwards to have so little confidence in his own virtue when he has earlier assured Harley that his "nature was never of that kind, that could think of getting rich at the expence of my conscience" (I, 171). Edwards's personality thus becomes submerged within the faceless character of a dialogist who serves first as Harley's strawman (he claims that the natives are better off under British rule than under their own princes) and then as a means of softening the brunt of Harley's attack on his countrymen.

The last fragment, "The Pupil," is the most artistic of these digressions. Though it begins with an aphorism, the exemplum that follows is much longer and more fully developed than the earlier notebook essays. The story of how young Sedley comes under the corrupting influence of Respino until he discovers, through the intervention of his tutor, his friend's crimes and hypocrisy is one of the many tales that Mackenzie interpolated into his novels. Though the elder Sedley is supposedly recollecting his own experience for Harley's benefit, having him do so is only a pretense for introducing the story since Harley shows no reaction whatsoever during or after the tale. Sedley appears in no other part of the novel, though twenty years later Mackenzie made him the hero of his only comedy, giving him a personality that clearly contradicted Sedley's earlier character.

We begin to see then the strong didactic bent that underlies Mackenzie's fiction: characters are frequently conceived in terms of ideas and attitudes, either as their spokesmen or as their illustrators. They may in fact be assigned didactic roles that conflict with their previously established personalities. *The Man of Feeling* is in some respects, then, an *anatomy*, to use Northrop Frye's useful term, because in part it "differs from the novel in its characterization, which is stylized rather than naturalistic, and presents people as mouthpieces of the ideas they represent."[40]

IV *Use of Pathos*

If Mackenzie is more concerned with voicing his ideas and observations than with investing his novel with a high degree of verisimilitude, he nevertheless does not permit such didacticism to override his predilection for pathos. Harley's denunciation of British imperialism is withheld, as we have seen, until Edwards has completed his story, discovered that his grandchildren have become orphans, and been settled on a farm. Harley's harangue becomes then an interlude, sandwiched in between incidents that relate to Edwards and those pertaining to Harley's jealousy, although the brutal treatment of the Indian native, as we have observed, would have offered a more natural and persuasive transition to his criticism. From such dissociation between thought and feeling stems much of Mackenzie's sentimentality.

A tale like old Edwards's is created almost entirely for its pathos. When Edwards and his family are forced to leave the lands his forefathers have farmed for generations, their old dog, Trusty, tries to follow them, but he is too weak to move far:

> "I called to him; he wagged his tail, but did not stir: I called again; he lay down: I whistled, and cried Trusty; he gave a short howl, and died!—I could have lain down and died too; but God gave me strength to live for my children."
>
> The old man now paused a moment to take breath. He eyed Harley's face; it was bathed with tears: the story was grown familiar to himself; he dropped one tear, and no more. (I, 163–64)

It might be said that Mackenzie is using the pathos of the scene to attack English social injustice were it not for the fact that Edwards's plight stems from such a variety of causes. A greedy landlord takes away the best of his farm in exchange for poorer land that Edwards finds too difficult to manage. When this circumstance is combined with a succession of adverse seasons and with the bankruptcy of the "corn-factor" who owed Edwards money, he is unable to pay his rent and is forced off the farm. Such a combination of natural and human evil, of deliberate cruelty and mere folly makes Mackenzie's purpose clear: Edwards's misfortunes, of which the death of Trusty is a poignant symbol, are devised less to illustrate a social evil than to evoke a strong emotional reaction. While our sympathy and pity are aroused because Edwards bears little responsibility for his plight and, therefore, suffers undeservedly, we devote relatively little thought to the conditions that bring about his downfall.[41]

In his first novel, Mackenzie's attention remains fixed upon the innocent victim of circumstances. Edwards, like similar paternal figures that appear in all Mackenzie's dramas, is simply another distressed father whose plight is calculated to arouse our pity.

In a revealing letter to his cousin, Mackenzie comments:

> I now send you the first Part of my favorite Passage, The Story of Old Edwards. There are some Strokes in it which I am prouder of than any thing I ever wrote. . . . It may be observ'd perhaps as a Sameness in me, that I so frequently draw aged Characters: and upon Recollection I own, there is scarce a Passage which particularly pleases myself in any Composition of mine, where this is not the Case. I somehow affix to Age the united Ideas of Tenderness & Dignity; & I naturally write what is easiest to me, that is what I am most pleas'd with; and hence my Propensity to the pathetic.[42]

Literature is judged rhetorically in terms of its affective value—the quality of a passage or scene depends upon its emotional impact on the reader. When Mackenzie forwarded Captain Atkins's story (Chapter XXIX) to his cousin, he warned her: "As the inclosed Chapter is also of the melancholy kind, let it not be read till you have a mind to indulge those Feelings which it endeavours to produce."[43] Such an approach to literature is, in fact, characteristic of Mackenzie's era; for, as René Wellek has pointed out, "the emotional effect which had always been the aim of rhetoric and of some poetry became under the influence of sentimentalism, the *sine qua non* of all poetry, even of all literature."[44]

In the loosely though delicately wrought confines of *The Man of Feeling*, Mackenzie found the right medium for indulging his love for pathos. The very laxity of his form encouraged a rhetorical approach toward his work. Incidents are staged and arranged in a way calculated to evoke a specific emotional reaction from the reader. Harley's visit to Bedlam, for example, is carefully organized to produce a series of successive responses leading to a poignant climax. Though he considers it an "inhuman practice" to exhibit the insane for the diversion of visitors, Harley is nevertheless induced by a friend to join such a tour. They are first shown the most violent and incurable inmates: "The clanking of chains, the wildness of their cries, and the imprecations which some of them uttered, formed a scene inexpressibly shocking. Harley and his companions, especially the female part of them, begged their guide to return" (I, 51). The scene is too shocking and loathsome to allow any response but fear and horror from the spectators and presumably the reader.[45]

They next visit the more harmless inmates, and Harley is offered a private tour by a "decent-looking man." He sees a mathematician, a speculator, and a schoolmaster, each of whom has gone mad because of some delusive obsession or quirk of fate. The situation is more comical than lamentable because each madman is totally absorbed in his former calling and seems unaware of his own condition. Harley is at this point relatively detached and concludes that "the passions of men are temporary madnesses; and sometimes very fatal in their effects" (I, 55). The discovery that his guide is himself an inmate who thinks he is "the Chan of Tartary" reinforces the comic tone of the scene as well as confirming Harley's ingenuous nature.[46]

Such a mood is, however, quickly dispelled when Harley's attention is aroused by a young woman in the female quarters of the institution: "Separated from the rest stood one, whose appearance had something of superior dignity. Her face, though pale and wasted, was less squalid than those of the others, and showed a dejection of that decent kind, which moves our pity unmixed with horror: upon her, therefore, the eyes of all were immediately turned" (I, 56). Here is a carefully wrought composite of all the elements evocative of pathos. Her sorrow "moves our pity" because it is restrained, even dignified. Little in her appearance undermines such an impression; indeed, her "pale and wasted" features help to increase our pity because there are few signs of abject poverty to repel us. As Anna Letitia Barbauld suggests, "a judicious author will never attempt to raise pity by any thing mean or disgusting. . . . there must be a degree of complacency mixed with our sorrows to produce an agreeable sympathy; nothing, therefore, must be admitted which destroys the grace and dignity of suffering; the imagination must have an amiable figure to dwell upon."[47]

The death of the girl's lover, whom her tyrannical father would not permit her to marry, has driven her out of her mind. Instinctively, she senses Harley's humanity and addresses him: "My Billy is no more! . . . Do you weep for my Billy? Blessings on your tears! I would weep too, but my brain is dry; and it burns, it burns, it burns!" (I, 58). Her frenzy and singing, reminiscent of Ophelia, is designed to sustain, even to intensify the pathos Mackenzie has built up. The chapter ends with Harley urging the keeper to " 'be kind to that unfortunate.'—He burst into tears, and left them."

Harley's meeting with the mad girl is obviously the climax to the whole Bedlam scene. The first two parts, one evocative of terror and one of humor, inhibit that compassion which Harley's initial observation has encouraged us to feel: "it [insanity] is a distress which the humane must see with the painful reflection, that it is not in their power to alleviate it." Our sense of pathos is thus all the more intensive when we are exposed to "The distress of a daughter." Yet, as with Edwards's story, emphasis is placed on the object of our commiseration rather than its cause. The girl is completely preoccupied with Billy's death and makes no mention of her Harlowe-like father who had tried to force her to marry a wealthy old suitor. Billy's death, moreover, is the result of a natural evil—a fever caught in the West Indies although his journey was undertaken in the hope of acquiring sufficient wealth to gain her father's approval.

At other times, however, Mackenzie integrates thought and feeling into an effective scene. Captain Atkins's story about how he returned home to find his daughter gone is told with restraint and simplicity: "I arose, and walked through the room. My Emily's spinnet stood, at the end of it, open, with a book of music, folded down at some of my favourite lessons. I touched the keys; there was a vibration in the sound that froze my blood. I looked around, and methought the family-pictures on the walls gazed on me with compassion in their faces" (I, 130). Similarly, it may be said, Mackenzie is touching the reader's "keys" in order to arouse his compassion. Our sympathy for Atkins is, moreover, all the greater since we already know the consequences of Emily's indiscretion—she has become a common prostitute. Yet, in this instance, the reader's emotions are not stirred up for their own sake but to drive home a moral lesson—Mackenzie is letting young women experience the anguish a father feels: "did they but know," exclaims Captain Atkins, "with what anxiety the heart of a parent flutters round the child he loves; they would be less apt to construe into harshness that delicate concern for their conduct" (I, 133).

V *Sensibility*

There appears, however, to be one drawback to such a technique: men differ in their capacity to sympathize with another person's feelings because, as we have said earlier, their response is contingent upon the delicacy of their own senses. The efficacy of the above scene thus depends upon the reader's sensibility. As Alexander Gerard points out in his *Essay on Taste* (1759), "*sensibility of heart* . . . fits a man for being easily moved, and for readily catching, as by infection, any passion that a work is fitted to excite. The souls of men are far from being alike susceptible of impressions of this kind. A hard-hearted man can be a spectator of very great distress, without feeling any emotion: A man of a cruel temper has a malignant joy in producing misery. On the other hand, many are composed of so delicate materials, that the smallest uneasiness of their fellow creatures excites their pity."[48] Literature thus takes on an esoteric quality: its salutary effects seem to operate only on the emotionally responsive reader. When Atkins embraces Harley in gratitude for having saved his daughter, the narrator exclaims: "We would attempt to describe the joy which Harley felt on this occasion, did it not occur to us, that one half of the world could not understand it, though we did; and the other half will, by this time, have understood it without any description at all" (I, 126). The implication is, however, that the reader obviously belongs to the "other half."

Mackenzie could make such an assumption because his audience had learned to prize sensibility as a sign of refinement and vied with each other for proof of emotional susceptibility. To possess sensibility was to be particularly favored by nature. As Hannah More expresses it, "Sweet Sensibility! thou secret power/ who shed'st thy gifts upon the natal hour, / Like fairy favors."[49] And, if such susceptibility brought with it a greater capacity to suffer, its possessors were more than compensated by the knowledge that their very grief testified to their sensibility. As an anonymous writer in *London Magazine* wrote: "if the heart be touched with a story of distress, it will at the same time experience a delightful sensation; and if the tears oftentimes flow, say, can you call it weakness? can you wish to be divested of this genuine test of tenderness, and desire the departure of Sensibility?" The very gratification we derive from pathetic compositions stems from the fact that they enable us to give proof of our sensibility: "the pleasure which arises from legends of sorrow, owes its origin to the certain knowledge, that our hearts are not callous to the finer feelings, but that we have some generous joys, and generous cares beyond ourselves."[50] Hugh Blair arrives at a similar conclusion in trying to account for our enjoyment of tragedy: "We are pleased with ourselves, for feeling as we ought, and for entering, with proper sorrow, into the concerns of the afflicted."[51]

Such assumptions help to explain the age's predilection for pathos as well as the popularity of *The Man of Feeling*.[52] Temperamentally inclined toward pathetic literature, Mackenzie exposed his readers to an array of tender scenes that exercised and taxed their sensibility. His novel soon became, in fact, a yardstick for measuring one's emotional responsiveness. The *Monthly Review*, though hardly inclined to praise the novel, had yet to concede that "the Reader, who weeps not over some of the scenes it describes, has no sensibility of mind."[53] A more enthusiastic reaction came from Mackenzie's friend, James Elphinston: "Intently hav I watched hiz [Harley's] recepcion," he wrote three weeks after the novel's publication, "az wel to' judge ov hiz receivers, az ov himself. In onnor ov boath, it rejoices me to' assure yoo, dhat evvery reader ov feeling haz received him az a broddher."[54] Under the circumstances, it is hard to estimate how honest and spontaneous the response to *The Man of Feeling* actually was, for the desire "for feeling as we ought" undoubtedly made many a reader's reaction more self-conscious than he would have cared to acknowledge. Indeed, we catch a glimpse of this phenomenon in a letter Lady Louisa Stuart wrote to Scott in 1826: "I remember well its [*The Man of Feeling*] first publication, my mother and sisters crying over it, dwelling upon it with rapture! And when I read it, as I was a girl of fourteen not yet versed in sentiment, I had a secret dread I should not cry enough to gain the credit of proper sensibility."[55]

Viewed from such a perspective, the novelist and his reader form a relationship of mutual admiration in which the reader's emotional response flatters both the author's artistic skill and the reader's own sensibility. We can see this process in action in a revealing exchange of letters in 1778 between Hannah More and Mackenzie. After playfully berating him for his lachrymose novels—"Really, in common justice, you owe me some compensation for the tears you have made me shed so frequently and so plentifully"—she admits that she is really in his debt: "for most precious to the heart of sensibility, is the sorrow excited by such causes! and I am savage enough to wish earnestly that I had talents and pathos to be even with you in the same way, and so take a short method to get out of your debt by breaking your heart."[56] Her compliment is as much directed at herself as at him because it attests to her sensibility, and Mackenzie knows how to respond in kind, though he boasts more openly: "We are perfectly agreed about the *pleasure* of the *pains* of sensibility; I may therefore say, without trespassing against the accuracy of a compliment, that I am proud of having had it in my power to confer that pleasure on you; but you are less in my debt than you imagine; though a man, and a man of business, I too can shed tears and feel the luxury of shedding them; your *Percy* has cleared scores between us in that respect." And he adds later: "Do write again, ... and (since you wish to break my heart) that I may have another opportunity of fooling at a tragedy. To some late ones I can reverse the answer given to Romeo—'God Coz, I had rather weep.'"[57]

With such a receptive audience and with a rhetorical theory of literature dependent upon the emotional manipulation of the reader, Mackenzie was led, not too surprisingly, into excesses of emotionalism that grate on modern ears. Sentimentality, in our pejorative sense of the word, is an almost inevitable by-product of a rhetorical view of literature since the writer's techniques for affecting the reader are bound to be colored by the changing modes of interpreting and responding to experience. Society and our immediate environment condition our reaction, and a scene that may have seemed fraught with delicate and natural feelings for one age may seem bathetic and ludicrous in another era. Lady Louisa Stuart, who read *The Man of Feeling* to a group of acquaintances some fifty-five years after its publication, confesses with surprise: "I am afraid I perceived a sad change in it, or myself—which was worse; and the effect altogether failed. Nobody cried, and at some of the passages, the touches I used to think so exquisite—Oh Dear! They laughed." The recollection of her former response to the novel leads her to "reflect on the alteration of taste produced by time. What we call the taste of the Age, in books as in anything else, naturally influences more or less those who belong to that Age, who converse with the world and are swayed by each other's opinions."[58]

The modern reader is particularly sensitive to being emotionally manipulated; though in a wider sense, as Wayne Booth has shown, all fiction is rhetorical since the novelist must control his reader's reactions if he is to accomplish his esthetic purpose. The difference is that Mackenzie, as we have seen, openly creates a scene to evoke a specific emotional response from his audience. He plays upon their sympathy just as Emily Atkins wins over her father by playing upon his pity:

His daughter was now prostrate at his feet. "Strike," said she, "strike here a wretch, whose misery cannot end but with that death she deserves." Her hair had fallen on her shoulders; her look had the horrid calmness of out-breathed despair! Her father would have spoken; his lip quivered, his cheek grew pale; his eyes lost the lightning of their fury! there was a reproach in them, but with a mingling of pity! he turned them up to heaven—then on his daughter.—He laid his left hand on his heart—the sword dropped from his right—he burst into tears. (I, 121–22)

The scene is undoubtedly melodramatic, the diction is hackneyed, the gestures stereotyped and theatrical. But we have no reason to believe that such lack of both originality and realism inhibited emotional involvement on the part of Mackenzie's reader. As we have already indicated, the *Monthly Review* claimed that anyone "who weeps not over some of the scenes it describes, has no sensibility of mind." The reviewer immediately adds, however: "But it is to be observed, that the knowledge of men it contains, appears to be rather gathered from books than experience." The juxtaposition of these two statements suggests that lack of verisimilitude does not necessarily prevent a reader from responding emotionally to a scene. He may have been conditioned through his reading to be moved by certain literary formulas and stock responses—by what may be called the *rhetoric of sensibility*. And such a conditioning process is all the more likely to operate in an audience that reads novels in order to cultivate and give testimony of their own emotional susceptibility.

VI *The Danger of Sensibility*

The risk always exists, however, that a reader will confuse the idealized world of such novels with reality and that pride in his own emotional responsiveness will make him as vulnerable to manipulation by the designing individual as by the novelist. In this case, sensibility, the basis for human sympathy and goodness, becomes a liability rather than an asset because its possession makes one an easier prey than a person of a more impassive temperament. Though Mackenzie did not emphasize this negative side of sensibility in his first novel, as he did in later works, the theme is suggested by Emily Atkins's story as well as by Edward Sedley's experience.

Emily, who possesses the emotional susceptibility and imagination to be strongly affected by plays and novels, is an easy victim when Winbrooke, a Lovelace-type rake, sets out to ensnare her. By pretending to share Emily's sensibility, he easily puts her off her guard and plays on her naïve idealism; as she relates, "I interpreted every look of attention, every expression of compliment, to the passion I imagined him inspired with, and imputed to his sensibility that silence which was the effect of art and design" (I, 105). Convinced by the testimony of her readings and her own temperament that the intensity of the emotions is a measure of their genuineness, she is unable to believe "that his expressions could be too warm to be sincere." Being endowed, moreover, with the sensitivity and taste to respond intelligently to literature makes her vain and vulnerable to flattery: "He asked my opinion of every author, of every sentiment, with that submissive diffidence, which shewed an unlimited confidence in my understanding" (I, 105).

By thus playing on her emotions, Winbrooke succeeds in seducing her: "If it is dangerous to be convinced, it is dangerous to listen; for our reason is so much of a machine, that it will not always be able to resist, when the ear is perpetually assailed" (I, 106). The impotence of reason as a force of moral restraint is a common theme of the eighteenth-century Scottish philosophers, one that is most persuasively stated by Hume: "Nothing can oppose or retard the impulse of passion, but a contrary impulse. . . . the principle which opposes our passion cannot be the same with reason, and is only called so in an improper sense. We speak not strictly and philosophically, when we talk of the combat of passion and of reason."[59] In *The Pursuits of Happiness,* Mackenzie expresses a similar idea:

> Men must have passions; paint them, if you can,
> Where less the brute enjoys, and more the man.
> To combat passion when our reasons rise,
> Reasons are better passions in disguise.
> In every climate, and in every age,
> With poet, priest, philosopher, and sage;
> Let pedant preachers smooth it as they will,
> They preach successful to the passions still;
> Direct the wish to rise, the tear to fall,
> Give fear to some, and vanity to all. (VIII, 72)

Edward Sedley faces a temptation that resembles in some respects Emily's experience. His corruption is only prevented because he has the good fortune to have a tutor who knows how to "preach successful to the passions." Sedley shares Emily's sensibility and naïve idealism: "I had ideas of virtue, of honour, of benevolence, which I had never been at the pains to define; but I felt my bosom heave at the thoughts of them, and I made the most delightful soliloquies" (I, 217). Like her, he too is enticed by signs of sensibility because he accepts them as tokens of virtue. Describing Respino and his friends, Edward speaks of "their wit, their eloquence, their warmth of friendship, and their sensibility of heart: 'And their honour,' said I, laying my hand on my breast, 'is unquestionable'" (I, 220). In reality, Respino's sensibility, like that of Joseph Surface, is limited to the language of sentiment: his actions are those of a callous libertine. As with Emily, sensibility can thus be used as a façade to deceive and corrupt those most susceptible to its influence.

Instead of "a lecture of sour injunctions," Mountford, Sedley's tutor, enlightens his charge and thus dissipates Respino's corrupting influence by exposing Edward to the victims of the latter's crimes—a family pining away in a debtor's prison because the wife refused to be seduced by Respino. The pedagogic principle that Mountford practices is defined in the maxim that precedes the tale: "let the feelings be awakened, let the heart be brought forward to its object, placed in the light in which nature would have it stand, and its decisions will ever be just" (I, 216). Mountford seeks to influence his pupil by exposing him to a carefully selected experience; and, in a sense, Mackenzie sees himself in a similar role vis-à-vis the reader. After a particularly emotional scene, the narrator of *The Man of the World* comments apologetically: "The reader will pardon the digression I have made; I would not, willingly, lead him out of his way, except into some path, where his feelings may be expanded, and his heart improved" (II, 187). Although such a purpose may underlie sections of *The Man of Feeling*, in much of the novel the prevailing mood of pathos is evoked, as we have seen, for its own sake.

CHAPTER 3

The Man of the World

THE *Man of the World* is without doubt Mackenzie's weakest novel. "This author," wrote a reviewer for the *London Magazine*, "describes well, but he seldom describes nature. He seems to be one of those idle and uninformed philosophers who study mankind in their closets."[1] Mackenzie, who himself felt uneasy about its publication, probably sensed its inferiority to his first work of fiction. "This Performance," he wrote to his cousin, "I confess I am more apt to be afraid than proud of; a second work is a dangerous thing, the falling off of an Author, like all other fallings off, being perhaps still more mortifying than the failure of the first attempt."[2]

At the outset of the novel, Richard Annesly defies his father, a wealthy tradesman, by choosing to become a clergyman instead of his successor in business. Disinherited, he marries a neighbor's daughter and retires to a country parish. After his wife has given birth to two children, she dies during the birth of a third, who soon succumbs to smallpox; and the surviving children, Billy and Harriet, grow up under the watchful tutelage of their father. As Harriet matures, she begins to attract the attention of Annesly's neighbor, Sir Thomas Sindall, who formulates plans to seduce her. Taking Billy under his wing when the boy enters Oxford, Sindall succeeds in corrupting the youth until he commits an armed robbery because of gambling debts, is arrested, and is finally transported to America for fourteen years.

By pretending to be Billy's friend, Sindall has meanwhile succeeded in ingratiating himself with his sister. Because his first plot to seduce Harriet fails, Sindall arranges to have her coach waylaid by "outlaws" from whose captivity he then pretends to rescue her. The subsequent events recall Samuel Richardson's *Clarissa Harlowe*, for Sindall, like Lovelace, drugs his victim before raping her. When Harriet returns home, she believes Sindall's promises to marry her and, therefore, rejects the marriage proposal of her father's old friend, Rawlinson. When she learns that she is pregnant, she is persuaded by Sindall's accomplice, Camplin, that her seducer is waiting nearby in order to marry her. Taken to the same house where she had formerly been raped, she learns that Sindall is unwilling to marry her but has arranged for Camplin to accept her. Terrified by this development, she goes into labor and is delivered of a girl. Upon the news of the death of her distraught father, Harriet weakens and becomes delirious. The final shock is the news that her baby and its nurse have apparently drowned. She dies; and Sindall, feeling some remorse, erects a monument over the graves of Annesly and Harriet.

The second part of the novel opens many years later. Sindall's family now includes his ward, a young lady named Lucy; his aunt, Mrs. Selwyn, a contentious and rather comical widow; and his cousin, Harry Bolton, a benevolent youth who is Sir Thomas's presumptive heir. Bolton and Lucy fall in love; and Sindall, who has designs upon his beautiful ward, obtains a commission for his cousin in a regiment in Gibraltar. While in London, Bolton saves the life of old Rawlinson, who had been Annesly's friend and who, as the executor of his estate, has vainly tried to find his son. Rawlinson soon dies, leaving to Bolton his large estate plus the trusteeship of William Annesly's patrimony. While Bolton becomes a model landlord, Mrs. Selwyn dies; and Sindall replaces her with the servile Mrs. Boothby, who is to help him seduce his ward. Lucy, however, is able to repel his first advances and soon after learns from him that she is not the daughter of Sindall's friend but a mere foundling. She escapes with the help of a servant only to be waylaid by Sindall and taken to a nearby house to accomplish his purpose. Meanwhile, Bolton, who has come to rescue Lucy, meets a soldier who turns out to be William Annesly, returned home after having lived for years among Cherokee Indians. Upon hearing screams from a nearby house, they rush in just in time to save Lucy from being raped. After Sindall has been wounded, the nurse enters. She, who had supposedly been drowned with Harriet's child, announces that Lucy is really Sindall's daughter, who had deliberately been left in his way the night he found her. Sindall dies repentant, and the lovers are finally joined in marriage.

Mackenzie described his second novel as a "contrast to the *Man of Feeling*."[3] If Harley represents an idealization of goodness in a callous and rapacious world, Sindall, as his name suggests, personifies much of its evil. Yet Mackenzie was not able to unify *The Man of the World* by the means he had employed before. The subtle tone that diffuses and harmonizes the often fragmentary scenes of his first novel could not be evoked by a story designed to depict the machinations and crimes of a villain. The form of *The Man of Feeling* had been developed, Mackenzie claimed, "partly from wanting to' shun dhe common rote ov novvels."[4] Now, however, he resorted to all the traditional devices of eighteenth-century fiction. Borrowing largely from Richardson, as well as from Oliver Goldsmith's *The Vicar of Wakefield*, he tried to create a Lovelace-type rake who preys upon two generations of a clergyman's family. The result is melodramatic and episodic because Mackenzie is more interested in evoking each bit of pathos from Sindall's victims than in providing his antagonist with adequate motivation.

I *The Nature of Good and Evil*

Like most rakes of eighteenth-century fiction, Sindall's libertinism is simply ascribed to the permissive nature of his upbringing: "he did what he liked, at first, because his spirit should not be confined too early; and afterwards he did what he liked, because it was past being confined at all." Harley's education, we should recall, was also neglected, but for a different reason. Their opposite natures seem to stem more from differences in temperament (as with Henry Fielding's Tom Jones and Blifil) than environment. Though Sindall's mother was "a very good woman, . . . he inherited none of her virtues" (I, 314).

Significantly, Sindall restrains his passions and behavior not by supposing himself the "impartial spectator" of his own actions but by an inherent shrewdness of character: "There was a degree of prudence, which grew up with him from a boy, that tempered the sallies of passion, to make its object more sure in the acquisition" (I, 314–15). Being completely selfish and pragmatic, he regards and cultivates other men's approval only insofar as it can benefit him. Since he cares not whether their praise is actually justified, Sindall is a most accomplished hypocrite; he has "that pliancy of disposition, that could wonderfully accommodate himself to the humour of every one around him" (I, 321),[5] a flexibility that gives him a marked advantage over the representatives of goodness. Harley, we recall, finds it impossible to accommodate himself to a rich relative because his "impartial spectator" abhors such opportunism—"the usual and expedient were terms which he held to be very indefinite" (I, 155).

Sindall is enabled to dupe men like Harley and Annesly, moreover, because their goodness tends to preclude the kind of shrewdness needed to penetrate Sindall's duplicity. In the world of Mackenzie's fiction, innocence and even naïveté are associated with virtue because, in interpreting other men's actions by the experience of their own feelings, the good are blinded to the machinations of evil.[6] When Sindall befriends Billy at Oxford, the Reverend Annesly's response is spontaneous and without suspicion: "His father, whom years had taught wisdom, but whose warmth of gratitude they had not diminished, felt the favour as acutely as his son; nor did the foresight of meaner souls arise in his breast to abate its acknowledgement" (I, 326).

Annesly's children, however, are Sindall's direct victims; and what I have characterized as the negative side of sensibility in reference to Emily Atkins and Sedley is more fully developed by Mackenzie in the corruption of Billy and Harriet. Both children are highly emotional, and Annesly is quick to recognize the assets as well as the liabilities of such temperaments: "To repress the warmth of temerity, without extinguishing the generous principles from which it arose, and to give firmness to sensibility where it bordered on weakness, without searing its feelings where they led to virtue, was the task he had marked out for his industry to accomplish" (I, 282). Like Mountford, the father appreciates the need to address the passions; but, when Billy is removed from his father's guidance, he is readily corrupted because Sindall also knows the advantage of appealing to the emotions.

To understand the basis for Mackenzie's psychological assumptions, we must turn once more to Adam Smith's *Theory of Moral Sentiments.* Man, Smith believes, possesses an inherent drive to seek his fellow men's approval: "Nature, when she formed man for society, endowed him with an original desire to please, and an original aversion to offend his brethren. She taught him to feel pleasure in their favourable, and pain in their unfavourable regard. She rendered their approbation most flattering and most agreeable to him for its own sake; and their disapprobation most mortifying and most offensive."[7] Such sensitivity to society's judgment (the "man without") is, however, only one part of man's moral nature: he must often disregard the "man without" if he is to act in a praiseworthy way rather than be merely desirous of praise. Nevertheless, this initial urge to gain other men's approbation molds his behavior since their reaction provides him with "the only looking glass" by which he gains an impartial view of himself and is able to develop "general rules of conduct."

An individual's moral development thus depends upon his environment—the values of his particular society are bound to help mold his self-judgment as well as his conduct. "For Smith," to quote A. L. Macfie, "morality develops through the historical growth of societies, and therefore relative to them; and the impartiality and information he defines as the standard depend on the socio-historical situation of the individual, on the view taken of his psychological motivation, and on his interpretation of 'fair play.' "[8] Such a concept, needless to say, is "the antithesis of an immediate moral sense declaring spontaneously yea or nay."[9] A society perverted by "custom and fashion" corrupts the individual who instinctively seeks its approbation: "Those ... who have had the misfortune to be brought up amidst violence, licentiousness, falsehood, and injustice; lose, though not all sense of the impropriety of such conduct, yet all sense of its dreadful enormity, or of the vengeance and punishment due to it. They have been familiarized with it from their infancy, custom has rendered it habitual to them, and they are very apt to regard it as, what is called, the way of the world, something which either may, or must be practised, to hinder us from being the dupes of our own integrity."[10]

Smith cites the reign of Charles II as an example of such a society, but he fails to evaluate his own age. Mackenzie, on the other hand, views his own period as degenerate and, therefore, as a threat to the individual's natural moral development. The Reverend Annesly, who, like Harley, has chosen a "sequestered life" and who frequently serves as the author's spokesman, has tried to isolate his children from such corruption. By making his son aware of the danger the world outside poses, he hopes to save him from its enticement:

> The two great movements of the soul, which the moulder of our frames has placed in them for the incitement of virtue and the prevention of vice, are the desire of honour, and the fear of shame: but the perversion of these qualities, which the refinement of society is peculiarly unhappy in making, has drawn their influence from the standard of morality, to the banners of its opposite; into the first step on which a young man ventures, in those paths which the cautions of wisdom have warned him to avoid, he is commonly pushed by the fear of that ridicule which he has seen levelled at simplicity, and the desire of that applause which the spirit of the profligate has enabled him to acquire. (I, 298)

Ironically, the minister's description is an all too accurate prognosis, for Sindall and his accomplices flatter Billy's ego by lavishing him with praise. As a result, he is reluctant to criticize their values even though he inwardly condemns them. Unable to oppose their arguments and fearing their ridicule, he pretends to approve what he as yet cannot accept: "Annesly's conviction was not changed; but the edge of his abhorrence to vice was blunted; and though his virtue kept her post, she found herself galled in maintaining it" (I, 329).

When Sindall has weakened Billy's "abhorrence to vice," the boy gradually becomes habituated to a profligate life. Yet Sindall is not satisfied until he has made use of Billy's compassionate nature to complete his victim's degradation. The woman who finally drives Billy to armed robbery is instructed by Sindall "to invent a plausible story of distress and misfortunes" to arouse his sympathy and later his lust. Amidst such folly, Billy's conscience becomes an "ungracious monitor," whose voice is ignored in spite of Reverend Annesly's former warning: "never suffer this monitor to speak unheeded, nor drown its whispers, amidst the din of pleasure, or the bustle of life. Consider it as the representative of that Power who spake the soul into being, and in whose disposal existence is!" (I, 312).

Billy's "monitor" or conscience, what Smith calls the "man within," is muffled by the intensity of his own passions. But, after Billy has robbed and been imprisoned, his conscience once more gains the ascendancy and he falls into despair, asking God to take back his life: "The passions which thou didst implant in me, that reason which should balance them is unable to withstand: from one only I receive useful admonition; the shame, that could not prevent, now punishes my crimes" (I, 397). By means of the "man within," he can once more imagine himself the spectator of his own behavior, and his remorse and despair stem from the horror of such a view. As Smith describes this reaction, "by sympathizing with the hatred and abhorrence which other men must entertain for him, he becomes in some measure the object of his own hatred and abhorrence."[11] Billy Annesly's plaint represents the dark side of sensibility and is Mackenzie's recognition that the emotions can be exploited to degrade man as well as used to ennoble him.

To a lesser degree, this doctrine is again illustrated in Harriet's downfall. Like Emily Atkins, she possesses that sensibility and imagination which can make her "weep all night from some tale which her maid had told of fictitious disaster" (I, 277). Though Annesly, as we have said, recognizes the potential danger inherent in such a temperament, his efforts fail to protect Harriet from Sindall's stratagems. Blind to Sindall's true nature because he feigns "those tender feelings, which were most likely to gain the esteem of the daughter" (I, 323), she easily comes to love him. His initial interest in her flatters Harriet's ego; and, though she "did not seriously think of Sindall as of one that was her lover, . . . she began to make such arrangements, as not to be surprised if he should" (II, 24–25).

Sindall's mock-rescue of her à la Sir Charles Grandison's genuine rescue of Harriet Byron, in Richardson's *The History of Sir Charles Grandison,* as well as his self-inflicted wound, recalling Lovelace's pretended illness, produces emotional reactions in Harriet that Sindall knows how to exploit. Though she shares no guilt in the actual seduction, since she is drugged, her subsequent actions attest to the intensity of her infatuation. She believes Sindall's promises of an early marriage because in spite of what has occurred, she is somehow still blind to his real character: "'The flattering language of his letters . . . soothed the tumults of a soul to whom his villainy was yet unknown, and whose affections his appearance of worth, of friendship, and nobleness of mind, had but too much entangled" (II, 91–92).

She meets Sindall's accomplice behind her father's garden, recalling Clarissa's meeting with Lovelace; and, just like her prototype, she is hardly able to walk to the waiting carriage that will carry her to her doom. But such Richardsonian touches are superficial at best, for Mackenzie's Harriet entirely lacks the depth of Clarissa's character and conflict. Whereas Richardson's heroine is torn by guilt and disillusionment after she recognizes that she has been capable of loving an immoral person, Harriet remains in love with the man who has raped her and remains infatuated until he himself rejects her. Considerations of expediency, as well as feelings of love and guilt, are blurred by Mackenzie to enable him to evoke his favorite mood of pathos. The result is a shadowy picture of suffering and passivity that has little resemblance to the realities of Harriet's situation.

If the forces of good prove weak and passive in the first part of the novel, they are more successful against Sindall in the second part only because fortune or, more precisely, Mackenzie begins to favor them. Sindall cannot entice Lucy as easily as he had ensnared her mother because his sudden change from guardian to lover disgusts and frightens his ward. Lucy, moreover, has an advantage Harriet lacked by being warned in time about Sindall's real intentions. Though Bolton, like Reverend Annesly, possesses too much goodness to recognize Sindall's evil nature until Lucy's letter finally enlightens him, he himself seems invulnerable to corruption. Bolton is, in fact, another "Man of Feeling" who has "a disposition instinctively benevolent, and an exquisite sensibility of heart" (II, 149).

As is the case with Harley, Mackenzie makes no attempt to account for Harry Bolton's goodness of heart. Indeed, the influence of Sindall should have had some corrupting effect on the youth, but nothing of the kind occurs. Bolton's inherent moral perfection is invulnerable because Mackenzie never allows him to be tempted. He encounters no Sindalls or Respinos either at the university or in London, but he has the good fortune to save the life of Rawlinson and thus inherit an estate of a thousand pounds a year.

II *Modes of Characterization*

By now, Mackenzie's means of delineating his characters is fairly clear: emotional susceptibility is the key to personality. He who has the sensibility and the concomitant imagination to respond deeply to a wide range of experiences possesses, if not an inherent disposition toward goodness, at least the potentiality to attain such a state of grace. His own sensitivity enables him to sympathize with the suffering of his fellow men; and, what is more important, it enables him to try to judge his own conduct from the perspective of an "impartial spectator." While such emotional susceptibility does make one particularly vulnerable to manipulation and corruption, it is likewise true that for a person of this temperament there is always hope of reformation when his passions have abated and the "man within" resumes his ascendancy.

On the other hand, the man who is too insensitive to react to anything but the grossest experiences is likely to prey on humanity because he lacks the sensibility to be compassionate. Moreover, his relative indifference to the ways in which other men judge him inhibits his moral development. His very inability to respond emotionally, however, gives him an immense advantage over his more sensitive fellow men. Having no strong emotions to deflect him from his goal or to limit his means, he can pursue his own selfish ends unhesitantly and efficiently, as does the gambler Blackbeard: "This man possessed an unmoved equality both of temper and aspect; and though, in reality, he was of no very superior abilities, yet had acquired the reputation both of depth and acuteness, from being always accustomed to think on his own interest, and pursuing with the most sedulous attention every object which led to it, unseduced by one single spark of those feelings which the world terms weakness" (I, 378–

79). Billy Annesly, no match for such an opponent, impulsively risks all his winnings on a challenge from Blackbeard, though he has previously lost everything to him and pawned his sword to recover his losses. When he again loses, "the transport of his passion could not express itself in words; but taking up one of the dice, with the seeming coolness of exquisite anguish, he fairly bit it in two" (I, 387).

Overcome by anger and remorse, Annesly can only give vent to his feelings through a spontaneous physical reaction. For Mackenzie, such a response characterizes the feeling part of society. When deeply moved, Harley, for example, becomes similarly inarticulate and physically responsive. When Miss Walton provides clothes for Edwards's grandchildren, Harley is at a loss for words: "There were a thousand sentiments; but they gushed so impetuously on his heart, that he could not utter a syllable" (I, 195). Sindall, on the other hand, is rarely at a loss for words; indeed, his very articulateness testifies to his lack of feeling and spontaneity. When Harriet weeps over Billy's departure, "Sir Thomas did not want for expressions of comfort or of kindness." In contrast, Jack Ryland, a kindly man, "had but few words to communicate his feelings by; but his eyes helped them out with an honest tear" (II, 47). Not surprisingly, Tom, the narrator, can also become inarticulate. When Annesly dies, he exclaims: "Sindall! and ye who like Sindall—but I cannot speak!—speak for me their consciences" (II, 117). When Annesly faints at the news of Harriet's pregnancy, his servant Abraham throws himself down beside him, "tearing his white locks" (II, 102). A poor woman who witnesses Lucy meeting with Miss Walton expresses her joy by crying and laughing "by turns" (II, 177).

Weeping is, of course, the most common physical response to a moving experience, as some of these examples indicate. Since tears presumably demonstrate one's capacity to be moved emotionally, they indicate some evidence of goodness even in a Sindall. When Billy entrusts Harriet to his care, he accepts his responsiiblity "with a tear; a tear, which the better part of his nature had yet reserved from the ruins of principle, of justice, of humanity. It fell involuntarily at the time, and he thought of it afterwards with a blush" (II, 44). Precisely because tears are considered involuntary do they take on such significance in Mackenzie's fiction: their presence is the one sign that can be trusted in a deceitful world. Harley believes in Emily Atkins because she weeps in response to his generosity: "There is virtue in these tears," he exclaims (I, 91). Likewise, Tom's reaction to Mrs. Wistanly's praise of Annesly immediately creates a rapport between them: "The tender solemnity of her look answered the very movement which the remembrance had awaked in my soul, and I made no other reply than by a tear. She seemed to take it in good part, and we met on that ground like old friends" (I, 254). Rarely, if ever, is the testimony of the lachrymal glands questioned. Tears are sacrosanct and somehow cannot be simulated by the insensitive part of mankind. In Ben Jonson's *Volpone,* Mosca can produce tears to hoodwink the innocent Bonario, but in Mackenzie's age such a stratagem is no longer permissible because tears have taken on too much significance.

As the hallmark of sensibility, an open display of tears is seen as a measure of a society's refinement. Tears suggest compassion and humanity, which Adam Smith has characterized as the "amiable virtues" that depend upon the ability "of the spectator to enter into the sentiments of the person principally concerned." In contrast, the "respectable virtues" of self-denial and self-control depend upon the ability "of the person principally concerned to bring down his emotions to what the spectator can go along with."[12] The precarious existence of a primitive people requires that they practice the "respectable virtues" for the sake of their own survival, but an advanced society, because of the security it offers, makes relatively few demands upon the individual's capacity for self-denial. Such security, however, encourages the "amiable virtues" since, "before we can feel much for others, we must in some measure be at ease ourselves."[13]

Because the individual in a refined society knows that he can expect his fellow men's empathy, he is more likely, Smith argues, to give vent to his emotions: "A humane and polished people, who have more sensibility to the passions of others, can more readily enter into an animated and passionate behaviour, and can more easily pardon some little excess. The person principally concerned is sensible of this; and being assured of the equity of his judges, indulges himself in stronger expressions of passion, and is less afraid of exposing himself to their contempt by the violence of his emotions." For this reason, Cicero "could, without degrading himself, weep with all the bitterness of sorrow in the sight of the whole senate and the whole people," while such an emotional display would have been considered an impropriety in the "earlier and ruder ages of Rome." France and Italy have long practiced such "animated eloquence," though it "is but just beginning to be introduced into England."[14]

III *The Cherokee Utopia*

It is no accident that William Annesly's expiation takes place among a group of Cherokee Indians, since his crime stems from "ungoverned passions." The tribe that he joins is impassive to pain and grief, condemning the kind of emotionalism that characterizes more civilized societies. When Annesly weeps at the approaching demise of the old chief who has adopted him, he is told that in those tears "there is no wisdom, for there is no use" (II, 301). Such contempt for any sign of sensibility stems, according to Smith's thesis, from the Indians' hazardous existence: "All savages are too much occupied with their own wants and necessities, to give much attention to those of another person. A savage, therefore, whatever be the nature of his distress, expects no sympathy from those about him, and disdains, upon that account, to expose himself, by allowing the least weakness to escape him.... The savages in North America, we are told, assume upon all occasions the greatest indifference, and would think themselves degraded if they should ever appear in any respect to be overcome, either by love, or grief, or resentment."[15] An Indian when captured thus "submits to the most dreadful torments, without ever bemoaning himself, or discovering any other passion but contempt of his enemies."[16] A similar account comes from Annesly, who witnesses the Cherokees' prisoners being tortured before undergoing his own "trial of fortitude" (II, 295–96).

Not surprisingly, Annesly extols this primitive way of life

since his own impulsive nature has brought him continuous misery. Because his existence among the Indians has taught him a type of stoic wisdom, he can bear the discovery of having been cheated out of his furs with calm resignation. As he tells Bolton, "let me warn you, from sad experience, to beware of those passions which at your age I was unable to resist, and which, in the commerce of the world, will find abundant occasion to overcome incautious and inexperienced youth" (II, 285). Bolton, of course, hardly requires such admonishment in this novel since, as we have observed, he is never exposed to the kind of temptation Annesly has had to face.

Yet, if Mackenzie continued to create such idealized "Men of Feeling," the more realistically drawn character of Annesly attests to a growing empirical approach toward man's moral nature. Though the stoic Cherokees scorn the ideals of sensibility, their way of life is described in idyllic terms that expose the author's own emotional involvement. It is a society "where greatness cannot use oppression, nor wealth excite envy; where the desires are native to the heart, and the langour of satiety is unknown; where, if there is no refined sensation of delight, there is also no ideal source of calamity . . . the inhabitants feeling no regret for the want of those delicate pleasures of which a more polished people is possessed" (II, 300). Mackenzie's Cherokee utopia is inspired by nostalgia—one bred on the recognition that its simplicity can never be recaptured amidst the complexity and decadence of an advanced culture. Their homogeneous community offers to Mackenzie an attractive alternative to a society in which "Men of Feeling" find themselves alien beings and in which "the great movements of the soul," the desire of honor and the fear of shame, have been perverted so as to corrupt the individual.

The Man of the World represents a shift in emphasis if not also in values. While Mackenzie's belief in the positive value of sensibility remains unabated, he evinces a growing recognition that such emotionalism may be a two-edged weapon. For Harley, heaven is conceived in terms of sensibility where the tender feelings are revered rather than scorned (I, 235); for Annesly, on the contrary, the stoic primitivism of the

Cherokees is an approximation of paradise—one that he leaves reluctantly for a civilization of "fraud, hypocrisy, and sordid baseness" (II, 306).

CHAPTER 4

Julia de Roubigné

MACKENZIE'S last novel was published in 1777 when he was only thirty-two years old. *Julia de Roubigné* is his best and most mature work of long fiction, for it shows an artistic control often lacking in his earlier novels, as a summary of its action reveals. By losing most of his wealth in a lawsuit, Pierre de Roubigné, the father of Julia, is forced to sell his paternal estate, leave Paris, and move into the country. His neighbor Count Montauban befriends Roubigné, falls in love with Julia, and asks for her hand in marriage. Julia rejects Montauban's offer because she already loves Savillon, a youth who grew up with her and who has gone to Martinique to make his fortune. When a sea captain brings the news that Savillon is to be married to the daughter of a rich planter, Julia still cannot feel any love for Montauban. Roubigné, meanwhile, is in danger of going to jail for unpaid debts; and his wife, critically ill, tries on her deathbed to persuade Julia to marry Montauban in order to save her father. The Count, however, gives up his suit; furtively pays Roubigné's debts; and confesses, when he is discovered to be the benefactor, that he had ceased courting Julia only for the sake of showing his friendship disinterestedly. Julia, overcome by her father's entreaties, accepts him although she still has misgivings about marrying a man she cannot love.

When the scene shifts to Savillon's arrival in Martinique, we learn that he also loves Julia but that neither has admitted being in love to the other. He has come to his uncle's plantation in the hope of becoming wealthy enough to win Julia's hand; and, when his uncle dies, he inherits the estate and returns to France, unaware that Julia has married. Julia soon learns that Savillon has returned and that he has remained single.

Her anguish arouses Montauban's suspicion; he quickly discovers Julia's former intimacy with Savillon, but is not aware of how innocent that relationship had been. When Julia is persuaded to meet Savillon for a last farewell, Montauban manages to read the letter and vows to kill them both after their meeting. Savillon escapes, but Julia is poisoned by her husband. Julia's confession of her innocent love for Savillon makes Montauban finally realize of how little Julia has been guilty. He grows delirious when Julia dies and later poisons himself. Savillon returns to Martinique "to shrink up from all the feelings of life, and look forward, without emotion, to its close."

The obvious similarities between *Julia* and Rousseau's *La Nouvelle Héloïse* (1761) have often been pointed out. In each novel, the heroine is in love with a young man whose lack of wealth and social position make marriage inconceivable. Each goes abroad (Savillon to Martinique, St. Preux around the world) while the heroines of both novels are reluctantly persuaded by their fathers to marry men whom they do not love. There are, however, important differences; while Julia's and Savillon's relationship remains chaste and innocent, Julie and St. Preux have an affair that leads to her pregnancy. Whereas Montauban is a passionately jealous and vindictive man who tries to kill Savillon, Wolmar, Julie's husband, is an impassive but benevolent man who invites St. Preux to join his household.

I *Realism*

The circumstances that led to the composition of *Julia* are related by Sir Walter Scott: "A friend of the author, the celebrated Lord Kames, we believe, had represented to Mr. Mackenzie, in how many poems, plays, and novels, the distress of the piece is made to turn upon the designing villany of some one of the *dramatis personae*." Mackenzie thereupon developed a story "in which the characters should be all naturally virtuous, and where the calamities of the catastrophe should arise, as frequently happens in actual life, not out of schemes of premeditated villany, but from the excess and over-indulgence of passions and feelings, in themselves blameless, nay, praiseworthy, but which, encouraged to a morbid excess, and coming into fatal though fortuitous concourse with each other, lead to the most disastrous consequences."[1]

Such a plan represented a radical departure for Mackenzie, since in his previous novel "the distress of the piece" had stemmed ultimately from the malevolence of an outright villain, Sindall, whose evil nature is a constant—there is as little attempt to account for his malice as there is to justify Bolton's goodness. In Mackenzie's third novel, however, he sought to create tragedy through the interaction of characters who were "all naturally virtuous." He was being urged to write a "moral tragedy," to use Lord Kames's own term, "where a story is purposely contrived to illustrate some moral truth, by showing that disorderly passions naturally lead to external misfortunes."[2]

In *The Man of the World,* Sindall is introduced with heavy-handed allegorical overtones: "It was thus the good man instructed his children. But, behold! the enemy came in the night, and sowed tares!" (I, 313). We have only to compare such a passage with Montauban's impressions as he plots his wife's murder to see the significance of Mackenzie's change: "I hear the tread of her feet in the apartment above. Did she know what passes in my mind!—the study in which I sit seems the cave of a demon" (III, 311). In place of a simplistic kind of black-and-white dichotomy, *Julia* presents us with the reality of subjective experience. Instead of a melodramatic struggle between good and evil, attention is focused on man's conflict with himself and the circumstances that lead him to choose the lesser good.

II *Narrative Technique*

The form of *Julia* reflects this new perspective, for, to capture the drama of introspection and self-conflict, Mackenzie turned to the epistolary novel, then at the height of its popularity,[3] which Richardson had perfected some thirty years before. *The Man of the World,* we recall, already shows the influence of *Clarissa,* but it consists of the kind of superficial borrowings characteristic of most seduction novels in the late eighteenth century. To reproduce Richardson's narrative technique of alternating points of view that tended to complement and contradict each other was much more difficult and hence more unusual.

Mackenzie uses three major epistolary narrators, Julia, Montauban, and Savillon, each of whom has a friend in whom he confides. Though there are no active respondents, as in *Clarissa* —only indirect allusions and occasional quotations from letters the correspondents have received—the letters possess, nevertheless, a remarkable sense of immediacy and verisimilitude. For Julia, writing to Maria "is only another sort of thinking" (III, 151); and Montauban feels that it would be "insincerity to a friend like Segarva, not to trust him with the very thought of the moment, weak as it may be" (III, 267). As a result, we get an internal view of the major characters that encourages us to relate to and believe in their reality.

At times the imitation of Richardson is slavish and obvious. Julia complains that Maria teases her about Montauban in a manner that recalls Miss Howe's talent for raillery, while Montauban angrily underlines passages in Julia's intercepted letter like Lovelace going over Miss Howe's letter to Clarissa. Such heavy-handed touches are overshadowed, however, by Mackenzie's superb use of Richardson's narrative technique. For Julia and Montauban, letter writing becomes an obsession—a means of capturing the elusive, transitory experience and fathoming its contradictions and ambiguities. At times, their monologues serve a therapeutic end (III, 332); in other instances, they lead to introspection and insight. As Montauban's suspicions about his wife grow, he begins to recognize what he has so long refused to admit either to his confidant or to himself:

> I have had time to think.—You will recollect the circumstances of our marriage; her long unwillingness, her almost unconquerable reluctance.—Why did I marry her?
>
> Let me remember. I durst not trust the honest decision of my friend [Segarva, his confidant], but stole into this engagement without his knowledge; I purchased her consent, I bribed, I bought her; bought her, the leavings of another!—I will trace this line of infamy no further: there is madness in it!
>
> Segarva, I am afraid to hear from you; yet write to me, write to me freely. If you hold me justly punished—yet spare me when you think on the severity of my punishment. (III, 289)

The reader has all along known the situation because alternating points of view have objectified his perspective and thrown an ironic light over the narrators' subjectivity. When Julia, concerned about whether Montauban has seen Savillon's picture on her dressing table, meets her husband, her report dramatically delineates her own state of mind. She describes his behavior, her subsequent response, and finally her analysis of that response: "When I went down stairs, I discovered nothing in his behaviour that should have followed such a discovery. On the contrary, I think he seemed more pleased than usual, and was particularly attentive to me. I felt his kindness a reproach, and my endeavours to return it sat awkwardly upon me. There was a treachery, methought, in my attempts to please him; and, I fear, the greater ease I meant to assume in making those attempts, I gave them only more the appearance of constraint" (III, 282–83).

Four pages later the same scene is described from Montauban's point of view. He has seen the painting, but he has decided to pretend ignorance until he has learned more. However, his emotions also betray him: "As I approached her, my heart throbbed so violently, that I durst not venture the meeting." A confrontation occurs soon after, and Montauban's narrative bears out Julia's fears: "I counterfeited as well as I could, and, I think, she was the most embarrassed of the two; she attempted once or twice to bring in some apology for her former appearance" (III, 288). Ironically, each misleads the other, though Julia acts unwittingly in arousing her husband's suspicion while Montauban's deception is deliberate. Such an inner view of the main characters inevitably arouses some sympathy in the reader. The kind of outright villain that Sindall exemplifies can usually be maintained only if we are denied access to his consciousness. If we are exposed to his thoughts and feelings, as we are to Montauban's, we are bound to feel some pity if not also fear from the possibility of falling into a similar misfortune.

III *Count Montauban*

When Julia first meets Montauban, she notes "something hard and unbending in the character of the Count": he has a "melancholy disposition" and carries honor "to a very romantic height" (III, 37–38). These qualities, in fact, bring about the eventual tragedy. His love for Julia seems to mellow his character so that she can write, "he has lost much of that sternness, (dignity, my father calls it,) which used to chill me when I approached him" (III, 55); but such a change is not lasting. After their wedding, Julia admits hesitantly that "Montauban seems to have resumed somewhat of his former dignity. . . . the ease of the husband has restored him to his native character" (III, 251). Aloof, inflexible, easily suspicious, he makes demands on his more sensitive wife like the Duke in Robert Browning's "My Last Duchess": "I would not have her pensive—nor very gay neither.—I would have nothing about her, methinks, to stir a question in me whence it rose" (III, 264). Thus he easily draws false conclusions from Julia's behavior and perused letters. Convinced that she is unfaithful to him, he becomes, like Othello, obsessed with jealousy, and plans revenge. Yet, ironically, his inability to hide his feelings from his wife prevents Julia from admitting her former attachment to Savillon: "His look had a sternness in it, so opposite to those feelings which should have opened the bosom of your distracted Julia, that I shrunk back into secresy, terrified at the reflection on my own purpose" (III, 304).

But, if Montauban's demeanor is austere and forbidding, it is partly due to his own wavering resolution. His doubts and fears must be suppressed for the sake of redeeming what he supposes is his tarnished honor. When he decides to read Julia's letter furtively, he senses his own moral degradation but insists that "the fate of Montauban is set upon this cast, and the lesser moralities must speak unheeded" (III, 296). He decides to poison Julia secretly to prevent her tears and protestations from affecting his resolution; but, after the deed is done, he begins to fear that Julia has been innocent. His own reflection alarms him as he begins to sense the enormity of his crime: "Methought some one passed behind me in the room. I snatched up my sword in one hand, and a candle in the other. It was my own figure in a mirror that stood at my back.—What a look was mine!—Am I a murderer?—Justice cannot murder, and the vengeance of Montauban is just" (III, 333).

Montauban, then, is no insensitive villain. Austere, inclined toward misanthropy, he is yet capable of admiring Julia's sensibility and falling passionately in love with her. This emotional capacity humanizes his character and arouses our interest. When he gives up his suit to win Julia in order to save her father from prison, both father and daughter acknowledge his self-sacrificing generosity. "I could not," he explains to Roubigné, "while I sought your daughter's love, bear the appearance of purchasing it by a favour; now, when I have renounced it for ever, I am free to the offices of friendship" (III, 139–40). No doubt he is sincere at the time, basking in the sense of his own magnanimity. Yet he has unconsciously hit upon the perfect strategy to win Julia, as he later recognizes himself: "I purchased her consent, I bribed, I bought her."

This is not to say that Montauban has until now been blind to Julia's motive for accepting him. When he wins her hand, he admits to his confidant that Julia's affection is based on gratitude rather than on pure love. But this fact, he argues, in no way degrades her feelings for him: "If they say, that affection is a mere involuntary impulse, neither waiting the decisions of reason, nor the dissuasives of prudence, do they not in reality degrade us to machines, which are blindly actuated by some uncontrollable power? If they allow a woman reasonable motives for her attachment, what can be stronger than those sentiments which excite her esteem, and those proofs of them which produce her gratitude?" (III, 148). Montauban is rationalizing, hiding from himself the reality of the situation: Julia has not changed her mind because his magnanimity has excited "her esteem." This respect was already his when she had refused his proposal: "She owned her esteem, her friendship: these are poor to the returns I ask; but they must be exchanged for sentiments more tender, they must yield to the ardour of mine" (III, 75). But such a change of heart has obviously not occurred—she has accepted him from a sense of obligation, from seeing her proud father humiliated by having to accept money from a friend without possessing the means to repay him, as Montauban realizes but does not want to admit to himself. He finds it convenient to argue against romantic love though he has admitted his own "ardour." As Julia points out, "his feelings are to be an apology for his suit, while mine are not allowed to be a reason for refusal" (III, 122).

IV *The Danger of Romantic Love*

Yet, if Montauban's repudiation of romantic love is a rationalization, it represents out of context a persuasive argument that throws light on Mackenzie's ambivalent attitude. Though the author's sympathy lies undoubtedly with his heroine, he recognizes the danger of relying too much on the emotions in matrimonial choices. In the letter in which he announces the impending publication of *Julia,* he admits to his cousin:

> I am every day more & more stumbled about the proper Education of your Sex; there is a bewitching Sensibility we are apt to encourage in them, which I begin to fear is often a very unsafe Guide thro' Life, & I am sometimes at Repentance myself, for having done even the little that was in my Power towards it's Encouragement. In Marriage (the most momentous of all Eras in a Girl's Life) it often leads them astray, either from [a] fastidious Nicety which cannot be pleased at all, or th[e] Delusion which is self-pleased without the Allowance of Rea[son] or of Prudence; and if once the romantic Disposition has fairly pictured it's Man, the Admonition of Parents, the Advice of Friends, & the Opinion of the World, do but serve to heighten the Colouring.[4]

Mackenzie's uneasiness about the didactic effect of his novels finds expression in Montauban's argument just as it does in Mrs. Boothby's advice to Lucy in *The Man of the World.* Like Montauban, she claims "that those are the happiest matches which are founded on the soberer sentiments of gratitude and esteem." Yet she too is unreliable, clad as she is in the role of the "wicked chaperone" who is trying to inveigle the heroine into the arms of her would-be seducer (Sindall). Both novels express Mackenzie's favorite theme of kindred souls destined for each other (Bolton-Lucy, Savillon-Julia), their union endangered by a rival "suitor" who lacks the lovers' sensibility.

To the idealistic writer, this pattern held an endless attraction; but, at the same time, the more pragmatic moralist in Mackenzie began to question its assumptions. In the essays of the *Mirror* and *Lounger,* the empirical side of Mackenzie predominated; but in *The Man of the World,* muffled though he is by Mrs. Boothby's unreliability, the moralist in Mackenzie already argues against romantic love in terms that clearly anticipate the periodical essayist:

> "There is, I know," rejoined Mrs. Boothby, "a certain romantic affection, which young people suppose to be the only thing that comes under that denomination. From being accustomed to admire a set of opinions, which they term sentimental, opposed to others, which they look upon as vulgar and unfeeling, they form to themselves an ideal system in those matters, which, from the nature of things, must always be disappointed. You will find, Miss Sindall, when you have lived to see a little more of the world, the insufficiency of those visionary articles of happiness, that are set forth with such parade of language in novels and romances, as consisting in sympathy of soul, and the mutual attraction of hearts, destined for each other." (II, 242–43)

The fact that Mrs. Boothby's critique of sensibility is proven wrong by the narrator's concluding assurance of the couple's happiness does not necessarily invalidate her thesis, nor does his reference to "souls formed for each other," which uses the very diction of romantic love Mrs. Boothby has been deriding. It merely demonstrates that such a principle is inoperative in the rarefied atmosphere of Mackenzie's novel.

For ulterior reasons, both Mrs. Boothby and Montauban argue against romantic love in order to bring into question the trustworthiness of the emotions. Their position, however, finds a more reliable defense in Julia's mother, for Mme. de Roubigné warns that the emotions "must not be indulged too far; they poison the quiet of our lives" (III, 91). Yet Julia cannot accept her mother's claim that "romantic affection" is only an illusion of youth; her feelings, she insists, are her conscience. Hence she asks her friend, "should I not be unjust to Montauban and myself, were I *now* to act against them?" (III, 67).

V *The Fallibility of the Feelings*

Julia is arguing for the integrity of her feelings as a guide for self-judgment. Being extremely sensitive and emotionally susceptible, she cannot conceive of loving a man who does not share her sensibility and tenderness. She prefers a "yielding weakness" to Montauban's "inflexible right," and events prove her preference to be correct. Her marriage is a disaster even before Montauban's jealousy is aroused, for she describes herself as "a wife, without a wife's affection, to whom life has lost its relish, and virtue its reward" (III, 279–80).

Ironically, Julia's inordinate sensibility not only foredooms her relationship with Montauban but traps her into accepting him in the first place. When her father describes how Montauban wept as he confessed the reason for giving up his suit to win Julia, Roubigné's anguish overcomes his daughter's will in a scene reminiscent of *La Nouvelle Héloïse*:[5]

"These tears, Julia, these tears of my friend!—Would I had met my dungeon in silence;—they had not torn my heart thus!"

Maria, mine was swelled to a sort of enthusiastic madness—

I fell at his feet.—

"No, my father, they shall not.—Amidst the fall of her family, your daughter shall not stand aloof in safety. She should have shared the prison of her father in the pride of adversity; behold her now the partner of his humiliation!" (III, 140)

Roubigné and, indirectly, Montauban are playing upon Julia's all too responsive emotions. Her instinctive empathy and her own sense of obligation and duty bring about an almost automatic reaction that she is powerless to inhibit, though she sees herself as "the silent victim of the scene." Once again we see Mackenzie's view of man's frailty—his inability to resist a concerted appeal to his emotions.

Though no conscious effort is made to deceive and corrupt Julia—as was the case with Emily Atkins and Harriet Annesly—she is nevertheless driven to choose the lesser good through her father's passionate appeal. Her feelings, which she calls her conscience, lead her temporarily awry because of the violence of her sensations. To quote Francis Hutcheson, one of the most influential of the Scottish moralists: "it is often observed, that the very best of our particular Affections or Desires, when they are grown violent and passionate, through the confused Sensations and Propensities which attend them, make us incapable of considering calmly the whole Tendency of our Actions, and lead us often into what is absolutely pernicious, under some Appearance of relative or particular Good."[6] Her fatal meeting with Savillon comes about through similar circumstances. Though she agrees to see him, she is hesitant and soon revokes her promise, just as Clarissa rescinds her plan to escape from her family with Lovelace. Yet Maria's entreaties joined to Savillon's are too much for Julia to resist; they play upon her love and compassion until she yields, though she senses the imprudence of her decision: "I will think no longer—This one time I will silence the monitor within me" (III, 312).

By now Julia has recognized and accepted the almost fatalistic consequences of her temperament: "Had I not felt, as I have done, half the ills I complain of had been nothing, and at this moment I were happy. Yet to have wanted such a heart, ill-suited as it is to the rude touch of sublunary things—I think I cannot wish so much" (III, 305). Amidst her misery and regrets, she has yet a curious pride in her sensibility regardless of the price she has had to pay for it. Mackenzie, no doubt, admires this emotional quality in his heroine, though he is cognizant of its liabilities and feels obliged to dramatize them.[7] His personal attitude toward marriage shows how closely Julia's ideals represented his own. More than a year before he completed the novel he had "sketch'd out some Time ago," he announced to his cousin his impending marriage: "Tho I am not vain enough to set much Value on a Heart which I have often felt subject to many Imperfections, yet I think I may say it is not every one to whom it would have yielded; there is a Delicacy, perhaps not always a happy one, which I believe it to possess, that could not have dispens'd, in the Object of it's Choice with something beyond the ordinary Class of Virtues, which having found, I trust, it will know how to value."[8] Though recognizing the fallibility of his feelings, Mackenzie, like Julia, prides himself in his sensibility and is willing to entail its risks. But, whereas he remains loyal to his intuitive judgment, his heroine compromises her own principles.

Julia's error lies in having permitted herself to be persuaded to marry a man whom she feels she cannot love—one whom she senses intuitively is incompatible to her. The fact that Savillon reappears unmarried adds a tragic twist to the story but does not really alter the central theme since Julia's happiness and peace of mind are already destroyed before his return. The point of Julia's tragedy was expressed earlier by the Reverend Annesly in *The Man of the World*; for, though he admits that "the violence which we have been accustomed to apply to love, is not always necessary towards happiness in marriage," he insists that "it is a treason of the highest kind in a woman to take him for her husband, whom a decent affection has not placed in that situation, whence alone she should choose one" (II, 82–83). Ironically, Julia herself echoes these sentiments early in the novel and foresees the tragic consequences of a loveless marriage, though she is overwhelmed by events later: "The suggestions I have heard of Montauban's unwearied love, his uncommon virtues winning my affections in a state of wedlock, I have always held a very dangerous experiment" (III, 121).

VI *The Martinique Interlude*

In his last novel, Mackenzie no longer seeks to glorify sensibility as such, though his admiration and sympathy for the feeling part of society remains unabated. The rest of mankind, however, is no longer regarded with condescending disdain, nor simply equated with materialism and moral inferiority. In August, 1773, six months after the publication of *The Man of the World*, he wrote to his cousin: "In the Midst of your own Sensations you must make Allowance for common Minds. The Self-Enjoyment of the Soul is not the Property of every one; & the Beauties of Nature & Culmony form but a mere Landscape to the Eye, when they are not a Stage for the finer Feelings to speak on & be heard. In this Article, at least, those are only capable of Delight who are deserving of it; and the *World of Sentiment* is not so entirely unsubstantial as the Votaries of the other are inclined to imagine it."[9]

Yet in *Julia* he has Savillon, another "Man of Feeling," write: "I begin to suspect, that the sensibility, of which young minds are proud, from which they look down with contempt, on the unfeeling multitude of ordinary men, is less a blessing than an inconvenience.—Why cannot I be as happy as my uncle, as Dorville, as all the other good people around me?" (III, 233). The "common minds" have become the "good people," and the "finer feelings" are now not necessarily a mark of merit and distinction. Although Savillon's dejection stems from the fact that his friend Herbert has sailed for England, we sense in him, as was the case with Julia, the recognition, nevertheless, that a refined emotional capacity is likely to condemn one to a degree of anguish from which less sensitive fellow men are spared.

Though the Martinique interlude, occupying some sixty-five pages, is largely irrelevant to the central story and weakens the novel, it illuminates by its very digressive nature Mackenzie's shifting ideas and values. While Julia's tightly knit tale did not easily offer him the freedom to stray from the main story-line, Savillon's experiences abroad provided Mackenzie an opportunity for such indulgence; in these letters, he suggests, *"it is not so much on story, as sentiment, that their interest with the Reader must depend"* (III, 180).

In Savillon's life on a West Indian plantation, Mackenzie once more explored the relationship between the "Man of Feeling" and an insensitive, profit-seeking world. In his first novel, we recall, the "misanthropist's" younger brother (representing the author himself) "experienced perpetual disgust" in the practice of law and eventually retired into the country on a small inheritance. Similarly, the Reverend Annesly finds the life of a tradesman so repugnant to his temperament that he willingly foregoes his inheritance for a small country parish. Savillon, on the other hand, instead of rejecting outright the commercial world, approaches it optimistically, hopeful of being able to humanize its crass materialism (III, 195). Shocked by the brutal treatment that Negro slaves receive, Savillon attempts to reform the system by demonstrating that a humane attitude on the part of the planters would bring them more profit. He frees the slaves in his charge and places them under the supervision of Yambu, a former native prince. Because they now raise sugar for the common good and "with the willingness of freedom," the Negroes accomplish twice as much work as before. By thus appealing to the profit-motive of the planters, Savillon seeks to prove that "self-interest will often be the parent of social obligation" (III, 196).[10]

Savillon's active involvement in life, as with Bolton, represents an important contrast to Mackenzie's first novel. Harley's reaction is to shrink from a corrupt society and retire "from the noise of the multitude," but Savillon tries to better "the multitude" by appealing to them on their own terms. Such a shift probably reflects Mackenzie's own changing perspective: the practical and idealistic sides of his personality, which had given his first novel its fine ambivalent tone, no longer seemed so irreconcilable. As he became a highly successful attorney in the Court of Exchequer, he naturally saw the everyday world of business in a more favorable light. The accumulation of wealth was not necessarily a sign of corruption, though the temptations were great. In May, 1773, three months after the publication of *The Man of the World,* Mackenzie admitted to his cousin: "I begin to alter my System a little of late, & to think Ritches a better thing than I once did. Nor is the Desire of Wealth alwise a hurtful one, if we can so contrive, as to forget it in the Acquisition, & to remember it only in the Disposal. This is not the most common method in the East Indies, nor indeed any where else."[11]

The solution was to humanize the commercial world by exposing it to the values men of sensibility offered. Savillon thus decries slavery not only because of its overt inhumanity but because it corrupts the slaveholder and his family: "from his infancy he is made callous to those feelings which soften at once and ennoble our nature" (III, 214).[12] Part of the answer, Mackenzie suggests in a later essay, is to give future businessmen a liberal education that would encourage the moral feelings: it would open "the mind to different motives of action, to the feelings of delicacy, the sense of honour, and a contempt of wealth."[13]

Savillon's uncle is exposed to the benign influence of his nephew's sensibility. Though skeptical of the latter's scheme and inclined to view his humanitarianism as romantic, he nevertheless consents to Savillon's experiment. On each side, an easy tolerance and respect exist that reflect Mackenzie's new perspective. The uncle, though he clearly lacks his nephew's emotional susceptibility, nevertheless admires it in Savillon: "he seems not displeased with my feeling what himself does not feel" (III, 198). The nephew, on the other hand, respects his uncle for his equanimity and an empirical judgment that is not "misled by feeling." The latter's sympathetically drawn character contrasts sharply with the callous representatives of commerce that the Reverend Annesly's father and cousin embody. Indeed, the degree of complexity and realism in this brief portrait of Savillon's uncle clearly stems from Mackenzie's abandonment of the simplistic characterization that had dominated his earlier novels. Lack of sensibility no longer precludes integrity and goodness of heart. Instead, what distinguishes the uncle from Savillon is a worldly cynicism combined with a well-meaning but often misconceived pragmatism, as his reaction to his nephew's scheme indicates.

But if Savillon can respect and feel affection for his uncle, their relationship can never reach the level of rapport that true "Men of Feeling" share. Beauvaris, Savillon's principal epistolary confidant, is another Harley—"his heart was not made for the world." Shy, self-effacing, he retired from a society that mistook his diffidence for indifference. Significantly, such a type now remains submerged through most of the novel—he never becomes an active correspondent nor is he specifically described until his death.

An equally important shift is noticeable in Mackenzie's manner of justifying those digressive episodes that find their way into all his novels. In *The Man of the World,* we recall, the narrator claims to lead the reader "into some path, where his feelings may be expanded, and his heart improved" (II, 187). In *Julia,* Mackenzie has become more apologetic and more candid about his motive. Introducing Savillon's account of his friend Herbert, he admits in a footnote: "the picture it exhibited pleased myself, and I could not resist the desire of laying it before my readers" (III, 217). Such changes are indicative of that new perspective toward sensibility which found its clearest expression in his *Mirror* and *Lounger* essays.

CHAPTER 5

Tales

THOUGH *Julia de Roubigné* is the best of Mackenzie's novels and demonstrates his growth as a writer, he was never fully at ease in this genre. The artistic control, the carefully planned and executed plot of a Richardson or a Fielding, Mackenzie failed to achieve. Perhaps he was looking back to his own works when he wrote in 1812, more than three decades after he had completed his last novel: "The only part of any great poetical composition, whether in the dramatic or narrative form, which no genius can produce in a hurry, is the plan and progress of the fable. On that the poet, gifted how much soever he may be, must often pause—must consider it in its general effect, as well as in its various parts in detail, in the relation which those parts bear to one another, as well as to nature and probability." But he then adds a revealing qualification: "yet I am rather of the opinion which I had once occasion to hear Garrick declare, that there is a power in exquisite writing to abate the faults, and to supply the wants of a defective plan; just as an excellent colourist can soften the error of his drawing, by the lights and shadows of his painting."[1]

Mackenzie's comparison is an apt one in reference to his own novels, for he is essentially a "colourist," a painter of subtle emotional scenes rather than a true novelist.[2] His concern for evoking a mood, particularly one of pathos, can override, as we have seen, considerations of unity and characterization. He is likely, in fact, to describe his novels in terms of a landscape painter: the characters in *The Man of Feeling* "are Figures of that mellow Colouring, on which, if they are tolerably drawn, we can look repeatedly with Pleasure; &, even when Misfortune is among 'em, it shades the Picture only with that Moonlight Gloom that makes Affliction lovely; in the other [*The Man of the World*], it is cover'd with the Darkness of a Storm from which we shrink with Horror."[3] It is not surprising, then, that in each of his novels he introduces digressions that depend "not so much on story, as sentiment."

But, if such a preoccupation with creating moods and eliciting emotional responses from the reader often weakened his novels, it had the opposite effect on his shorter pieces of fiction. The tale was Mackenzie's métier, and he made probably his most important contribution to English literature with it. "It is as the unassuming writer of tales," wrote Leigh Hunt, "that MACKENZIE has obtained just reputation. In a simple pathetic story he is never excelled, perhaps never equalled by any British writer."[4] The genre, which Jean Francois Marmontel had done much to perfect and popularize with his *Contes Moraux* (1761), offered Mackenzie an opportunity to create those simple but carefully developed scenes of pathos that most suited his temperament and talents. Immensely popular, his tales were among the most frequently reprinted stories in eighteenth-century miscellanies.[5] Though he included brief sketches in many of his essays and wrote two short tales, "Nancy Collins" (*Mirror,* No. 49) and "Albert Bane" (*Lounger,* No. 61), his best work is found in his longer stories.

I *"Story of La Roche"*

The best known of Mackenzie's tales is "The effects of religion on minds of sensibility. Story of La Roche," which appeared in *Mirror,* Nos. 42–44, June 19–26, 1779 (IV, 175–207). Popular enough to have been reprinted eight times by 1805,[6] the story concerns a Swiss pastor named La Roche who, while traveling with his daughter through France, is taken ill in a small town and is cared for by a noted English philosopher. Though an "unbeliever," the philosopher develops a warm friendship with La Roche and accompanies him back to his mountain village. Three years after his visit, the news of Mlle. La Roche's impending marriage brings him again to her father's parish. However, instead of her marriage he comes upon her funeral procession, for she has died of a broken heart after her lover has been killed in a duel. La Roche's capacity to hold fast to his simple religious faith in spite of this tragedy moves the philosopher, and he "wished that he had never doubted."

The philosopher, according to Mackenzie's later admission, is modeled on David Hume. In Mackenzie's *Life of John Home,* he describes Hume, when in company, as tactfully avoiding controversial aspects of his philosophy: "His good nature and benevolence prevented such an injury to his hearers; it was unfortunate that he often forgot what injury some of his writings might do to his readers."[7] Hume, he felt, was doing unaccountable harm with his philosophical skepticism because he was undermining men's religious faith. Mackenzie believed in a pragmatic weighing of advantages—belief in the necessity of belief was a self-evident maxim.[8] As he wrote to his cousin in June, 1770,

> exclusive of every Argument, from foreign Proof, or intrinsic Evidence, of it's Truth, I would be allow'd only to apostrophize to the Heart of an Infidel on Behalf of that System which he endeavours to overturn.—
>
> —"You profess, it is your Boast to profess, that Love to Mankind is your ruling Principle; but your Philanthropy is surely forgotten, when you would beat down that Pillar which supports the Feebleness of Humanity:—let me [stay][9] the Cruelty of your Purpose—pluck not his little Treasure from the Bosom of Poverty! take not his Crutch from Age, his Solace from Affliction! Our Way is but rugged at best; we trod it however lighten'd by the Prospect of that better Country to which we trusted it would lead; you tell us, that it will break off in some Wilderness, which Fancy may fill up as She pleases, but Reason is unable to delineate:—leave us not thus dark & comfortless; allow us to believe that our Virtue shall not be in vain; quench not the Hope it gives us of Immortality!"—[10]

A few years later, Mackenzie has a modified version of these words spoken by Reverend Annesly as a paternal exhortation to his departing son (I, 296–98). In "La Roche," these ideas are the central theme.

The story is divided into three parts, each focusing on the pastor's response to an experience. Yet, although the nameless philosopher is largely a spectator to these events, he rather than La Roche is the protagonist of the story. Mackenzie's main concern is with the psychological effect the pastor has upon the philosopher, and he delineates this process with remarkable indirection and restraint. In the first section, the philosopher witnesses La Roche's recovery. Viewing his restoration to health as a divine gift, the pastor prepares to carry out God's will "not as a duty, but as a pleasure." Without such faith, he claims he would have doubts about whether his recovery would prove to be "a real good." The philosopher tactfully acquiesces, but hastily changes the subject.

In the second part, the party reaches the pastor's village; the familiar scene recalls the recent death of Mme. La Roche to the man and his daughter. The father comforts the weeping girl, lifts his eyes to heaven, and quickly recovers his composure. "The philosopher," we are told, "interpreted all this; and he could but slightly censure the creed from which it arose." We learn nothing more directly, but the philosopher significantly insists on attending La Roche's evening prayers although he had earlier avoided a similar gathering when the pastor had offered thanksgiving for his own recovery. During the service, the daughter's hand falters on the organ, and her sobbing is heard from behind the curtain. La Roche loses his composure, but "his warmth overcame his embarrassment. He addressed a Being whom he loved, and he spoke for those he loved. His parishioners catched the ardour of the good old man; even the philosopher felt himself moved, and forgot, for a moment, to think why he should not."

In the last part of the story, the philosopher again sees a bereaved and suffering La Roche; yet, amidst grief for his dead daughter, his fervent faith consoles him and enables him to exhort his parishioners by the testimony of his own example: "while you see me suffer, you may know also my consolation." But it is the philosopher who is most affected by La Roche's dramatic sermon and by his later personal plea to him, which recalls Mackenzie's letter to his cousin: "if there are any who doubt our faith, let them think of what importance religion is to calamity, and forbear to weaken its force; if they cannot restore our happiness, let them not take away the solace of our affliction." The philosopher's "heart was smitten," and the remembrance of La Roche haunted him through the years, making him wish "that he had never doubted."

Though now convinced of the efficacy of religious faith, the philosopher cannot attain it himself since he lacks the requisite emotional susceptibility. La Roche's belief is as much dependent upon sensibility as was Harley's instinctive sympathy. The pastor, as the tale's full title indicates, is another "Man of Feeling," though seen in a religious context: "The ideas of his God, and his Saviour, were so congenial to his mind, that every emotion of it naturally awakened them." The philosopher, on the other hand, by the very nature of his work has lost this sensibility if his type of mind ever possessed it.

Yet such insensitivity, as with Savillon's uncle, no longer precludes a benign disposition: "if he was not easily melted into compassion, it was, at least, not difficult to awaken his benevolence." What distinguishes him from La Roche is an inability to respond emotionally to an experience. When they come upon towering, snow-capped mountains, the philosopher can only view them scientifically and "murder to dissect." La Roche, however, speaks of the sublimity of the scene and the ideas it arouses that lead him to a contemplation of its Creator. For him, the sense of God's presence is an intuitive awareness with which Nature has endowed him, just as it has given him an appreciation of natural beauty and music. The philosopher, La Roche suggests, has been denied the capacity to feel God's influence, just as he has been deprived of an ear for music. Though Mackenzie remains deliberately ambiguous about the relationship between sensibility and philosophy, the implication is fairly clear that the latter stifles emotional susceptibility. As Savillon points out, "Knowledge or learning . . . sometimes [is] fatal to taste, if by taste is meant the effect which beauties have on ourselves, rather than the power of criticising on that which they ought to have on others" (III, 241).

Such anti-intellectualism is not really surprising when we consider that Mackenzie's "Men of Feeling" are characterized by their innocence and their reliance on sensibility.[11] The philosopher is charmed with La Roche and his daughter because "he found in them the guileless manner of the earliest times, with the culture and accomplishment of the most refined ones. Every better feeling, warm and vivid; every ungentle one, repressed or overcome." The two characters thus combine the innocence of an idyllic golden age with that refinement of human nature which, for Mackenzie, characterizes the best part of an advanced society.

What makes this story so memorable is its deceptive simplicity. The events are described in a low-key, matter-of-fact tone and possess a natural unity that is never undermined by extraneous incidents. Associations are developed in one part of the tale in order to be utilized suggestively in the following section. The scene of the daughter playing the organ behind the drawn curtain comes to haunt La Roche's memory when, after her death, he sees the open curtain and the silent instrument; her faltering, unfinished performance has come to foreshadow her own demise. Another image, a light moving in the night and reflected by the dark waters of a lake, appears as a "piece of bridal merriment" to the expectant philosopher until proximity turns it ironically into remnants of the daughter's funeral procession. After this revelation, the scene shifts naturally to the pastor himself, seated in his dimly lit church before his parishioners: "La Roche sat, his figure bending gently forward, his eyes half-closed, lifted up in silent devotion. A lamp placed near him threw its light strong on his head, and marked the shadowy lines of age across the paleness of his brow, thinly covered with gray hairs." The portrait is strongly dramatic and underlines the pathos of the moment. At the same time, the lighting is suggestive of La Roche's public role, of his will to turn his private grief into an exemplary stance before his people.

II *"Story of Louisa Venoni"*

"Story of Louisa Venoni" appeared in *Mirror*, Nos. 108–09, May 20–23, 1780 (V, 55–57). It explores a very different subject from that of its predecessor. On a journey through Piedmont, Sir Edward, injured when his horse falls, is nursed back to health by a peasant named Venoni and his daughter Louisa. Sir Edward soon falls in love with Louisa, who shows a degree of refinement much above her station. She is to be married to a rich but vulgar neighbor; and Sir Edward, taking advantage of her repugnance for such a match, offers to make her his mistress since his pride will not allow him to think of marrying so far below his station. Louisa, too mild mannered to rebuke him for his affront, can only weep. Finally, he overcomes her resistance by playing on her love for him, and they hurriedly depart for England. At Sir Edward's estate, Louisa, overcome by remorse but never reproaching her seducer, silently languishes. Finally, the plaintive tone of a hand organ arouses her attention, reminding her of her native valley. The organist, invited to play for her, introduces a melancholy air that Louisa had herself written; and the organist is revealed to be Venoni himself. Instead of condemning Sir Edward, he arouses his pity with his grief for his lost daughter. Sir Edward, who has already been torn by remorse and has realized Louisa's superiority over women of his own class, offers to marry her and is accepted.

In its seduction motif, the tale is reminiscent of Harriet Annesly's situation as well as Emily Atkins's story. But, whereas Sindall and Winbrooke only pretend to possess sensibility to help them seduce their victims, Sir Edward actually has much of the warmth and tenderness of a true "Man of Feeling." Like his namesake, Edward Sedley, from whom he may be descended, Sir Edward has a wise mentor to guide him while traveling abroad; and only after illness has forced his friend to abandon him does Sir Edward succumb to vice. Now, however, there is no simple villain like Respino or Sindall to mislead the hero and mitigate his guilt; instead, Sir Edward falters because he is too weak to resist the values of a corrupt society, the "man without," although the "man within" condemns them: "he was the fool of words which he had often despised, the slave of manners he had often condemned." Though he succeeds in persuading Louisa to elope with him, he fails to take into account his own better nature. Acting out a libertine role that he himself despises, he is torn by self-conflict: "His heart was not made for that part which, it is probable, he thought it could have performed: it was still subject to remorse, to compassion, and to love."

As in "La Roche," Mackenzie is concerned with the psychological effect one person can have upon another. Louisa, like the pastor, possesses both the innocence associated with a primitive society and the refinement of an advanced one. Born in the pastoral setting of a Piedmont valley, she is educated above her station by an upper-class lady; the combination of these qualities captivates Sir Edward and later makes him recognize his own folly. He leads Louisa astray by playing upon her fears of having to yield to her father's will as well as by exploiting her affection and pity for him, describing his own future without her in those terms of despair that are the stock-in-trade of the eighteenth-century rake. Louisa is too overcome by her feelings to resist such a stratagem for long; but, ironically, when they reach England, she unwittingly grasps a similar weapon by playing upon his feelings. Because it is against her nature to reproach him and because she senses her own guilt, she can only suffer passively. Such a response is, however, the one most calculated to affect a sensitive man like Sir Edward: "the quiet and unupbraiding sorrows of Louisa, nourished those feelings of tenderness and attachment."

Imperceptibly at first, his relationship with Louisa begins to assume the respect and delicacy of a sincere courtship. An infatuation that has been based on pride of conquest and possession develops into a need for and love of Louisa for herself: "In the society of Louisa he found sensibility and truth; her's was the only heart that seemed interested in his welfare." Sir Edward's changed outlook is an emotional reaction that stems from feelings of guilt and a sudden recognition of Louisa's true worth. As such, this change reflects again Mackenzie's belief that human improvement depends upon an appeal to man's "better passions." As he writes to his cousin, "he, who has Feelings to be awaken'd may be often guilty of Follies; but we have Grounds of Reclamation which we can urge with Satisfaction."[12]

The plebeian maiden reforming the aristocratic rake is, of course, a common enough theme in eighteenth-century fiction. Pamela, like Louisa, is educated above her class; and her would-be seducer also comes to prefer her to the women of his own class. Similarly, Louisa's dilemma of being threatened with having to marry a rich but boorish suitor is reminiscent of Clarissa's situation.

Mackenzie's main source for his tale, however, is Marmontel's "Lauretta."[13] The two plots are quite similar although there are important differences in Mackenzie's handling of the story. While

Marmontel embellishes the basic situation with long, often superfluous scenes and descriptions, Mackenzie, consistently economical, conveys by implication and suggestion what had been spelled out literally by his predecessor. Marmontel's narrator is frequently didactic in a heavy-handed way; Mackenzie's storyteller, assuming a more sophisticated audience, remains much more neutral though omniscient. On the other hand, Louisa and Sir Edward are far more noble-minded than Lauretta and the Count de Luzy. Whereas Louisa senses her folly as well as her guilt and instinctively rejects the temptation of wealth, Lauretta easily rationalizes away any personal responsibility and eagerly embraces the wealth and sensual pleasures Luzy offers her. Similarly, the Count shows little of that self-conflict which makes Sir Edward's later reformation believable. Luzy's belated offer to marry Lauretta is a means to round out the tale rather than a prepared-for psychological development. Nor is the reader readier to accept Lauretta's instant remorse once her father has discovered her: "The intoxication of love, the charms of pleasure, had banished the thought; but as soon as the veil was fallen off, she saw herself such as she was in the eyes of the world, and in the eyes of her father."[14] Marmontel's handling of the seduction theme is more naturalistic and hence more modern, but his blatant didacticism undermines such an impression, and he does little to counteract the melodramatic element inherent in the tale. Mackenzie avoids this danger by focusing attention on his protagonist's inner conflict and change of heart rather than on external events.

III *"Story of Father Nicholas"*

"The power of corrupt society and false shame over the natural feelings of virtue. Story of Father Nicholas" appeared in *Lounger*, Nos. 82–84, August 26–September 9, 1786 (VI, 238–73). Reprinted ten times by 1806,[15] it tells the story of a Benedictine monk and the tragic events that made him renounce the world. As young man, Henry St. Hubert comes to Paris with Delaserre, the rich son of a neighboring family. Because St. Hubert fears ridicule, his companion is able to lead him astray. However, after Delaserre has introduced him to Santonges (Delaserre's cousin) and to Emilia, the good man's daughter, he leaves to join his regiment, while Santonges's virtuous example restores St. Hubert's "natural disposition to goodness." In the winter, Santonges goes to Paris for his health and dies there, leaving Emilia to St. Hubert's care. The two soon marry and return to the Santonges estate in Picardy; but, when Emilia's first child is to be born, St. Hubert insists on taking her to Paris to ensure the best medical care. A boy is safely delivered; but, while the mother recuperates, St. Hubert again encounters Delaserre, who introduces him to a group of swindlers; they, by means of the seductive Mme. de Trenville, fleece St. Hubert of his money and estate. In desperation, he decides to kill himself and his family, only to falter when his sleeping infant son involuntarily clasps his finger. He flees Paris; later, after having lain ill at an inn, he meets a young painter who had drawn a portrait of his wife and child. From him he learns that the shock of his departure has killed his wife, their son succumbing with her. Torn with guilt and remorse, St. Hubert joins a nearby Benedictine monastery and becomes Father Nicholas.

The story's title, "The power of corrupt society and false shame over the natural feelings of virtue," suggests an affinity with "Louisa Venoni." Like Sir Edward, St. Hubert finds it hard to reject society though he senses its depravity. The difference is that Sir Edward finds the courage to renounce its values before he loses Louisa, while St. Hubert gains the necessary resolution only after Emily has died. Neither possesses that inner direction which enables Harley to ignore the ridicule and contempt of society: "let us not be slaves to the names it affixes to motive or to action." St. Hubert, on the contrary, is its reluctant servant because he fears its mockery: "I was ashamed of virtues to which I was naturally inclined, a bully in vices which I hated and despised."

St. Hubert's gradual corruption recalls Billy Annesly's fate—in fact, the Reverend Annesly's admonition is as applicable to St. Hubert as it is to his son: youth is misled because society has perverted man's innate "desire of honour" and "fear of shame." Delaserre, like Sindall, has only to play upon these "movements of the soul" to accomplish his purpose; but his success is made easier by what St. Hubert calls his "extreme sensibility of shame, which could not stand against the ridicule even of much inferior men." Likewise, both young men are seduced by seemingly virtuous women who reject them once they have shorn them of all their possessions.

When we compare the two treatments of this theme, "Father Nicholas" appears, however, as a far superior literary work. In part, this is due to the fact that the approximately fourteen years that had passed since the composition of *The Man of the World* had turned Mackenzie into a far more polished and accomplished craftsman. Nor must we overlook the confining demands of serial publication: for Mackenzie, who was inclined to digress and to interject, such necessary compression proved a salutary effect. Most significant, the superiority of "Father Nicholas" stems from its narrative perspective. In *The Man of the World,* Mackenzie had created a narrator totally sympathetic to the Annesly family and equally hostile to Sindall. Tom's emotional outbursts and didactic comments create a sentimental tone that helps to turn the novel into melodrama. Mackenzie, in short, lacked the narrative perspective through which to detach himself from his subject. In "Father Nicholas" he avoids this weakness by use of a retrospective narrator who recounts his own tragedy.

An elaborate narrative frame prepares us for St. Hubert's story. The narrator, residing for a few weeks in a Benedictine monastery, notices the austere figure of a monk of "a very superior order." Father Nicholas, he is told, "is of all the brotherhood the most rigid to himself, and the kindest to other men." When the old man later relates his tale of "laudable feelings perverted, of virtue betrayed, of false honour and mistaken shame," his account is colored by that remorse and self-mortification through which he hopes to atone for his sins. A lifetime of retrospection has made him a severe judge of his own youthful follies. This severity gives his narrative a restraint, even at times a matter-of-fact tone; but, at the same time, his account is highly dramatic since the old monk is careful to keep in check his foreknowledge and superior wisdom as he relives his experience. Mackenzie thus achieves an organic balance between his dramatic and retrospective narrators.

We are introduced to Mme. de Trenville, for example, through St. Hubert's limited point of view; but we also learn (what he could not have known at the time) why he proves to be such a gullible victim: "When silent, there was a certain softness in it [her countenance] infinitely bewitching; and when it was lightened up by the expression which her conversation gave, it was equally attractive. We happened to be placed next each other. Unused as I was to the little gallantries of fashionable life, I rather wished than hoped to make myself agreeable to her. She seemed, however, interested in my attentions and conversation, and in hers, I found myself flattered at the same time, and delighted." By such means we are induced to make our own emotional response and to draw our conclusions instead of being bullied into a reaction by a zealous narrator.

The way Mackenzie came to write "Father Nicholas," he tells us, is that on a visit to France in 1784, he caught sight of a family along a Picardy road:

> in the course of my walk, I came up near a very handsome villa, with a gentleman and a lady (I suppose his wife) and two or three beautiful children walking on the road . . . I was so struck with the pleasant countenance of both, not like the French, but with finer complexions and fair hair, that I could not help making a bow on passing them, and patting the head of one of the children, a beautiful boy. The gentleman welcomed my salute with a benignant smile from him and his lady. When I got to Paris and saw the frivolity and dissipation that prevails there, I thought of the contrast of situation between this country gentleman and his charming family living on his estate in the country, and that which, if he came to Paris and joined the fashionable circle there, he might naturally fall into; and thence personifying that seemingly happy pair, I wrote the story of *Father Nicholas.*[16]

The theme of rural innocence versus urban corruption is an all too common literary theme, and Mackenzie worked it into his story at every turn. In the country, St. Hubert's academic success distinguishes him, while Delaserre's efforts bear no fruit. In Paris, the latter triumphs because "his superior wealth enabled him to command the appearances of superior dignity and show." Delaserre can, in fact, only corrupt his victim in the city; in the country, his influence is more than offset by the good people—Santonges and Emilia; and, of course, the villain has nothing but contempt for rural life and manners. All misfortunes, moreover, take place in the city: both Santonges and his daughter die in Paris.

Yet, in spite of Mackenzie's claim to the contrary, "Father Nicholas" is far more than an attempt to depict the evils of urban life. Ironically enough, the simplistic deduction he draws from seeing that "happy pair" on the road is quickly dispelled by the succeeding experience: he learns that anyone caught violating the gentleman's game preserve is sentenced to the galleys. Society is as liable to corrupt the individual in the country as in the city: " 'Good God!' thought I, 'can this be so? Could that sweet couple with whom I conversed near yonder chateau, with whose physionomies [*sic*] I was so much charmed, send a fellow-creature to the gallies for killing a partridge or pheasant!—Yet, *je ne scais pas,* custom and the example around us do so change the nature, extinguish humanity, and harden the heart.' "[17]

As we already know from the title, "The power of corrupt society and false shame over the natural feelings of virtue," Mackenzie is once more concerned with the psychological factors that lead the individual to corruption. Though Mackenzie undoubtedly stacks the cards to demonstrate the evils of the city, there are good reasons why Delaserre's influence over St. Hubert increases in Paris. Because such a metropolis attracts profligates of every description who share Delaserre's vices, his values become naturally more alluring to St. Hubert. Delaserre's "contempt for any profession but that of arms" is reinforced in St. Hubert's mind once they arrive at the capital: "The *fierté* of every man who had served, the insolent superiority he claimed over his fellow-citizens, dazzled my ambition, and awed my bashfulness."

Once Delaserre has persuaded St. Hubert to give up his plans to join the Church, he induces him to share his life of dissipation. Yet St. Hubert's enjoyment of such pleasure is mere pretense designed to cover up his sense of guilt. Fear of ridicule thus turns him into a hypocrite who feigns to derive pleasure from what he inwardly despises while shamefacedly hiding every act of his better nature: "I was self-denied, beneficent, and virtuous, by stealth; while the time and money which I had so employed, I boasted to my companions of having spent in debauchery, in riot, and in vice." Yet such duplicity is fraught with danger, for use almost can change the stamp of nature. By becoming accustomed to vice, a man's repugnance and sense of guilt are gradually dissipated: "The habits of life . . . into which I had been led, began by degrees to blunt my natural feelings of rectitude, and to take from vice the restraints of conscience." As Mountfort warns at the end of *False Shame,* a comedy in which Mackenzie once more explores this theme, "he who is first such a hypocrite from vanity, or from fear, will be in danger of becoming, in truth, the character he personates."

The tales Mackenzie composed for the *Mirror* and *Lounger* brought to maturity his craft as a writer. Confined to a narrow canvas by the demands of serial publication, he conveyed by implication and suggestion what he had been often wont to represent with heavy-handed prolixity. Low-keyed in style and economical in the construction of his plots, he fixed his attention on psychological growth and change to produce a group of exquisitely wrought stories that represent a significant contribution to English fiction.

CHAPTER 6

Dramas

IF Mackenzie's temperament and talents were ideally suited for the composition of short fiction, they proved to be a decisive liability in the writing of tragedy. His plays, instead of revealing dramatic conflicts, merely present characters and situations capable of eliciting poignant emotional responses. Mackenzie's protagonists are exemplary figures who bear little responsibility for their plight, while his antagonists are ambiguously drawn villains whose motives and behavior are never realistically accounted for. Only in his one comedy, written more than fifteen years after he had completed his last tragedy, does Mackenzie produce good theater. Within the comic form of *False Shame*, he found the detachment and restraint that enabled him to transcend his own artistic limitations.

I Virginia

Much of Mackenzie's first play, *Virginia; or, The Roman Father*, was written when he was about sixteen years old although it was not completed until eight years later.[1] Though the play was never performed on the stage, Mackenzie in old age distributed a few privately printed copies among his friends.[2] The story is derived from Livy's *History of Rome* (III. XLIV–XLVIII), which Mackenzie followed fairly closely. In the play, the decemvir Appius develops a passion for the maiden Virginia, daughter of the plebeian soldier Virginius. Appius's freedman, Appulinius, hits upon a scheme to obtain Virginia by claiming that she is not Virginius's daughter but a child who was born to a female slave of his house and who was later lost. However, growing fearful of how the common people will respond to such outright trickery, Appulinius advises his master first to try "gentler methods." By promising to reward Virginius for past services and by recalling his brother from exile, Appulinius is convinced that the old soldier will cooperate and sacrifice his daughter. But Virginius disdainfullly spurns the offer and makes plans to kill her if there turns out to be no other way to save his daughter's chastity. Having recognized that Virginia is in love with Lucius, the son of his dead friend, he tries to prepare the latter for the loss of his love. Lucius, however, misinterprets Virginius's hints and imagines that he has accepted Appius's offer. In an effort to save Virginia, he persuades her to marry him immediately.

Meanwhile, Appius has fallen back upon Appulinius's first scheme to win his prey. Summoned to the forum, Virginius sees Appius rule against him and about to seize Virginia. He stabs his daughter mortally and makes his way home. Virginia, though dying, follows him and blesses her father before she dies. Lucius, confronted by his dead bride, kills himself in despair. The play ends with the news that the people, aroused by the death of Virginia, have rebelled and killed Appius.

In the privately printed version of the play, Mackenzie took notice of its weaknesses: "The plan of the play is miserably defective; and there is too much declamation and narrative, with too little incident or action."[3] It would be unwise, however, to dismiss *Virginia* as an insignificant piece of juvenilia bearing little resemblance to his later plays. His second play, *The Spanish Father*, is in many respects a reworking of *The Roman Father*; and Mackenzie's basic approach to tragedy, his mode of characterization as well as many of his ideas and values, is in fact already apparent in his first play.

In Livy's account, Appius himself devises the stratagem by which to gain possession of Virginia: "The plaintiff [Marcus Claudius] acted out a comedy familiar to the judge [Appius], since it was he and no other who had invented the plot."[4] Mackenzie, however, turns Marcus Claudius into Appulinius, Appius's freedman and evil genius, who contrives the schemes to satisfy his master's lust. The change is important because it reveals a type of characterization that recurs in each of Mackenzie's tragedies: there is always a figure of authority who uses his power unjustly against the heroine and her father or lover. However, such an antagonist is never a simple, straightforward representation of evil; his actions are always beset by qualms, by memories of his former goodness or resolutions to reform. Violently passionate, he depends upon the guidance of a cooler spirit to provide him with the means to attain his objectives. In essence, it is the degree of emotional responsiveness that distinguishes these two types of evil.

In a soliloquy that opens the second act, Appius voices his contempt of man's moral nature:

> . . . I have little of that thinking weakness,
> Which wisdom tells us wanders o'er the past,
> Gathering ambrosia from remember'd Virtue,
> And to the souls of Tyranny and Guilt
> Their horrors sending and remorseful pangs; (17)

Yet if he has freed himself from the restraints of an active conscience, his inordinate hate of Virginius suggests, nevertheless, an uneasy recognition of his own corruption. The truth is that Appius, as Virginius informs us, "once had virtue" but was corrupted by being entrusted with power. As Virginius recalls, the youthful Appius used to visit him to hear him recount his military adventures:

> Then, with the bare recital of some action,
> Oft would his haughty spirit rise, and speak
> Its fiery language from his rolling eye,
> Then would he act the scenes that I rehearsed,
> Grasp an imaginary sword, and stretch
> His muscles near to bursting with force
> Of fancy'd effort on a giant foe. (24)

In Appius a highly developed imagination is combined with an impetuous nature that brooks no restraint. His pride and ambition have debased his native goodness of heart to the point where he calls even his pretense of friendship for Virginius "this ill-becoming softness." Being highly emotional, moreover, he is easily manipulated by more sober and craftier men. Though Appulinius has not gained the control over his master that Alvarez and Hassan possess in Mackenzie's later tragedies, *The Spanish Father* and *The Prince of Tunis,* nevertheless, Appius's lack of shrewdness makes him dependent upon his freedman's "cool advices." The latter easily dissuades Appius from his rash plan to have Virginia seized at night by suggesting "other means / That bear less danger on them—" (6).

But, if Appulinius is his master's superior in his shrewd, practical approach to life, he is yet incapable of understanding a man of Virginius's principles. Blinded by his own cynicism, he assumes that the old soldier can be bribed into sacrificing his daughter. Appius, on the other hand, though he now scorns virtue, can still believe in its reality on the basis of his own former experience (19). We see, therefore, two representations of evil emerging, ones that are further developed in later plays and that influenced Mackenzie's fiction. One is both insensitive and unimaginative, cool and restrained because he has no violent emotions with which to contend. Such a *villain of principle,* as Mackenzie later calls him, may be said to be a villain *on* principle since he pursues his own self-interest unhesitantly without self-deception or guilt. Heedless of the means to attain his objective, he is, like Sindall, eminently cunning—a quality that for Mackenzie frequently denotes the antithesis of sensibility and moral idealism. The *villain of passion,* on the other hand, is too irrational and intemperate to be very artful, for, being highly emotional, he is frequently beset by feelings of guilt and remorse. Appius, though he momentarily recognizes the futility of pursuing mere sensual pleasure, never undergoes a reformation because Mackenzie makes no real attempt to develop his character. He disappears from the stage before the middle of Act II, after which we are given only indirect references to his presence. Attention is focused instead on the heroic figure of Virginius, the Roman father, just as it later centers on Alphonzo in *The Spanish Father.*

To establish Virginius's nobility of character, Mackenzie relies not only on the heavily sententious speeches of the character himself and the testimony of his friends but on confronting his hero with the temptation that had originally been offered to his daughter. In Livy's account, Appius tries to "seduce her with money and promises,"[5] while in Mackenzie's play the father faces such a choice. Yet the outcome is never really in doubt, considering Virginius's exemplary nature. He is revolted by Appius's attempt "to bargain for a daughter's honour" and resolves to kill her rather than permit Virginia's chastity to be compromised. Thus there is no real conflict but merely the highly emotional situation of a father's natural reluctance to kill his daughter (54–55).

In his earliest play, Mackenzie's overriding love of pathos is already apparent. As he later recalls, he used to recite this part of the play: "One scene in it I used to act myself, having a great passion for spouting, that in which Virginius meets his daughter after resolving rather to kill her than to allow her to be the slave of Appius. It might be partiality in those friends before whom I acted it, but they gave it tears as well as praise."[6] For Mackenzie, the tears of his friends attest to his success because he has been able to move their feelings. This rhetorical approach to literature, this concern not with the total dramatic potentiality of a situation but only its power to evoke a specific emotional response from an audience, mars all of Mackenzie's tragedies. The point is all the more true in the case of Virginia, whose largely passive role is designed to arouse our pity. Like all of Mackenzie's later heroines, her sensibility is quickly established by her propensity for tears. As she explains to her father:

> Thy picture moves me! yet I often weep,
> I scarce know why; methinks I would not wish
> To help that weaknes; 'tis my common sign
> Of joy, of sorrow, pity, admiration! (32)

Since she shares Virginius's ideals, no conflict can arise from the fact that she needs to die for the sake of her honor. Virginia, in fact, blesses her father for having stabbed her. Inner tension stems instead from her misinterpretation of Virginius's intentions. Convinced that he will sacrifice his daughter to Appius, Lucius tries to persuade Virginia that her only salvation lies in being immediately wedded to him. Virginia, believing Lucius's supicion, is torn between obedience to her father and her love for Lucius.

Their love developed, according to Silia (Virginia's attendant), in early childhood before they could understand their feelings for each other:

> When, fresh from Nature's hand, the colder ties
> Of sallow interest and unfeeling prudence
> Reach not our hearts, the softer cords that link
> Congenial spirits mark'd you for each other. (14)

The concept of "kindred souls" destined for each other comes, as we have seen, to be one of Mackenzie's favorite themes. It recurs in *The Man of the World* and *Julia de Roubigné* as well as in *The Prince of Tunis*. Genuine love depends somehow upon a relationship established in the innocence of childhood before experience has weakened the reliability of our feelings. Such "congenial spirits" obviously possess sensibility and their union is always endangered by a rival "suitor" who lacks their refined emotions. Appius serves a role that is later reenacted by Sindall, Montauban, and Barbarossa, while Lucius's character foreshadows in some respects Bolton, Savillon, and Arrasid.

As Virginia's lover, Lucius naturally shares her emotional susceptibility: "Thou knowest I [Virginia] love to weep for pity oft; / Thou too art gentle, Lucius, thou art wont / To paint the tender feelings in thy look" (34). In contrast to Appius, who has been corrupted by his inordinate passions, Lucius is a man of refined feelings and noble ideals. Magnanimity, he argues, depends upon sensibility rather than a resolute will:

> 'Tis not unfeeling reason, iron valour,
> The cold conclusions of a steady heart,
> That nurse the generous purpose; in the soul,
> That knows the melting change of softer passions– (22)

Such idealism finds expression in his spontaneous sympathy for his fellowmen, which has earned him the friendship of a Tuscan slave (27).

Mackenzie's basic mode of characterization is, then, already apparent in his first dramatic effort. Yet, if *Virginia* is of critical interest for the light it sheds on his development as a playwright and as a novelist, it is a poor and highly derivative work as a drama. The characters possess little realism or depth, and the play lacks unity of purpose. Because Virginius's character is too idealized, no real inner conflict can arise to weaken his resolution to kill his daughter. The ending, as in Mackenzie's later tragedies, is deliberately designed to create an emotional crescendo of shock and pathos. Instead of dying immediately (as is the case in Livy's account) from being stabbed in the heart, Virginia is allowed to walk home so that she can die on stage in her father's arms. Lucius, who originally lifts up the body of Virginia to arouse the people against Appius, now stabs himself to death beside the lifeless body of his bride.

II The Spanish Father

Mackenzie based his play *The Spanish Father* on a well-known Spanish legend. In the early eighth century, while the Goths ruled Spain, their general, Count Julian, invited and assisted the Saracens to invade Spain in order to revenge himself against his king for having ravished his daughter. Though there is no direct evidence, Mackenzie may have derived his story from an account in Voltaire's *Essays upon the Manners and Spirit of Nations.*[7] Whatever the immediate source of the play, we are told that King Rodriguez accidentally meets Ruzalla while her father, Alphonzo, is leading the Spanish forces against the Moors in Africa. An infatuation begins and, after several secret rendezvous, Rodriguez succeeds in seducing Ruzalla. As the play opens, Alphonzo is returning to retire from military service. Ruzalla, melancholy and remorseful, is able to awaken Rodriguez's sense of honor, and he agrees to marry her. However, Alvarez, his evil advisor, succeeds in dissuading him by raising doubts in his mind about Ruzalla's virtue and by inciting his anger against her proud father. Alphonzo, meanwhile, learns from her attendant that his daughter has met the King and forces Ruzalla to confess her secret meetings. He confronts Rodriguez with this evidence; and when the King angrily boasts of having seduced her, Alphonzo strikes him and is arrested and imprisoned in a dungeon. His jailer conveniently turns out to be Pedro, an old retainer, who promises to free him, while his friend Savedra brings news that Alphonzo's followers have begun a rebellion to overthrow the King. Ruzalla, confronting her father to plead permission to stay and suffer with him, is spurned and renounced by him. Later, freed from prison, he visits his daughter in order to remove her dishonor by killing her. He hears Rodriguez coming and stabs his daughter; in his ensuing clash with the King, both are mortally wounded. Before the victorious rebels enter, all the principal characters have died.

The Spanish Father was never performed on the stage. In his collected *Works*, Mackenzie recalls: "Garrick saw this play, and I had some conversation with him, when accidentally in London in 1775, on the subject. Among other doubts, as to its success in representation, he stated, as the strongest, that which arose from the nature of the catastrophe, which he thought too horrid for the stage" (VIII, 205). As Thompson has suggested, Mackenzie probably discussed the play with Garrick in 1773 rather than in 1775; for on January 5, 1773, William Robertson, the author of *Charles V*, had written a letter to introduce Mackenzie to Garrick: "He was so much convinced by your remarks that his former tragedy [*Prince of Tunis*] was not so perfect as he would wish any piece to be that appears on your theatre, that he has begun to work upon another subject, and will be glad to submit the sketch of it to your judgment."[8] The play was also submitted to John Philip Kemble, the noted actor and theater manager, who felt that "it was not well adapted for the Stage."[9]

Though Robertson implies that Mackenzie had begun a new play, considerable evidence indicates that he was actually revising the original version of *The Spanish Father*, which may have been written much earlier. On February 19, 1772, he wrote to his cousin: "I had plann'd a Tragedy myself on a celebrated Spanish Story which I left off upon the Recollection that it would run too near the Line of this Play [*The Fair Penitent*] of Rowe's, which is so perfect in its Way as not to leave Room for another to encroach on it's Department!"[10] In that Rowe's Sciolto, like Alphonzo, seeks his daughter's death to redeem her honor, the two plays do show a striking similarity; but this factor in itself does not disprove the possibility that Mackenzie was referring to another "Spanish Story."

But how are we to account for the fact that in the introduction to the play Mackenzie justifies his idealization of Alphonzo by ascribing it to "the enthusiasm natural to youth"? Even if he showed the play to Garrick in January, 1773, rather than in 1775, he was still unlikely to have considered himself a youth at twenty-seven.

He admits, moreover, that a character such as Alphonzo "in unskilful hands, is sometimes apt to develope itself in bombastic expression. There was a good deal of such expression in the first copy of this play, which, even at that time, I had taste enough to be sensible of. I find several passages of that sort, in the scroll now before me, which, though they possessed some poetical beauty, I had struck out, as going beyond the simplicity of nature, and the style appropriate to the situation" (VIII, 206). Again, it is hard to imagine that "unskilful hands" would refer to the author of the highly successful *Prince of Tunis.*[11] It seems more likely that Mackenzie is alluding to some period during the 1760's, after much of *Virginia* had been written. Once composed, the original manuscript of *The Spanish Father,* including its deleted passages, may have then been put aside without Mackenzie's making any attempt to have it staged. However, after *The Prince of Tunis* had been completed and accepted for performance in Edinburgh, Mackenzie probably returned to his earlier play, rewriting and perhaps altering parts of it in the hope of getting it staged before a London audience.

Whether such revisions prompted him to place the play after *The Prince of Tunis* in his collected *Works* or whether he was simply reluctant to admit that he had tried to get his tragedy produced as a new work, it is difficult to ascertain. Certainly, *The Prince of Tunis* is a more complex and ambitious play than *The Spanish Father.* The latter, as we said earlier, is to be seen as a reworking of the basic situation in *Virginia.* Several lines from his first play reappear, in fact, almost unchanged in *The Spanish Father.* Virginius recalls his wife's death to his daughter:

> she clasp'd my hand in hers,
> And pointing where in guileless innocence

> You lay and slept beside her, gazed upon me—
> And died without a groan! (32–33)

just as does Alphonzo:

> She grasped my hand,
> And, pointing where thy infant innocence
> Lapped thee in sleep beside her, gazed upon me,
> And died without a groan! (VIII, 283)

The basic difference between the two plays arises from the fact that, while Appius represents only a physical threat for Virginia, Rodriguez constitutes a psychological one, since Ruzalla's infatuation with the King brings about her seduction. It was necessary, therefore, to draw Rodriguez more sympathetically than Appius in order to justify the heroine's attraction; but Mackenzie was reluctant to encourage an audience to admire a man of Rodriguez's immorality. In a later essay, *Lounger*, No. 28, he questions the wisdom of such a strategy: "Lovelace is made a character which the greater number of girls admire, in order to justify the seduction of Clarissa." To solve this problem, Mackenzie set about refining the pattern he had already established in *Virginia*. Like Appius, Rodriguez is conceived as an impulsive man of authority who is easily swayed by his crafty counselor. But, whereas Appulinius only provides his master with the means to gain his objectives, Alvarez actually determines his King's goals by playing upon his emotions, thus serving to mitigate Rodriguez's guilt (VIII, 212).

Alvarez is the true villain of principle. More fully developed than Appulinius, he is cynical and pleasure loving but also callous and guileful so that he can easily deceive and manipulate more frank and impulsive natures. Reminiscent of Shakespeare's Iago, he is an egotistical and ambitious opportunist who owes loyalty only to himself. After Alvarez has artfully dissuaded the King from marrying Ruzalla, he bares his motives in a revealing soliloquy:

> So, I have touched him in the very part
> That pride and passion wince in; but Alphonzo,
> Whose temper suits my scheme, will gall him there,

> Even into madness: as for this Ruzalla,
> His general estimation of the sex
> Will I so aid, by colouring to my purpose
> Her weakness to himself, that he shall hold
> Her beauty at a rate of easy purchase.
> Her haughty sire, like some malignant power,
> Has checked my growing fate, and kept it down;
> But here, I trust, he falls. Alvarez then
> Shall stand secure, and Spain confess her lord. (VIII, 241–42)

Rodriguez is no match against such cunning. He is described as "open, / Generous, and brave; but rash and unrestrained / In passion's or in pleasure's warm career" (VIII, 212). Like Appius, easily swayed by his emotions, he lacks the sagacity to recognize Alvarez's duplicity and is, therefore, readily dominated by him. Ruzalla can awaken the King's sense of duty to her because he is inherently generous and unsuited to the role of a callous villain. Such efforts prove fruitless, however, because Ruzalla is no match for Alvarez's strategy. First, he arouses the King's distrust of Ruzalla's virtue for yielding to him, though Rodriguez was her tempter; second, he suggests that marriage with her would imply fear of her imperious father. He thus plays upon the emotions of the insecure and hence vulnerable Rodriguez, who is easily dissuaded from his former resolution: "I give my idle passion to the winds. / I am a king again" (VIII, 240).

By these means, much of the responsibility for the tragedy falls upon Alvarez, though Rodriguez becomes a weak and poorly conceived character. His conflict between sincere love and selfish expediency is never clearly delineated. When he makes his first appearance, he claims to be puzzled by the fact that Ruzalla has failed to meet him since her seduction; and he seems surprised by her distraught state of mind. Since we have no inner view of his character, it is difficult to ascertain whether Rodriguez's reaction is the product of insensitivity or the ploy of strategy. He is, in any case, blind enough to Ruzalla's real personality to try to make her his mistress, though her rebuke brings on an immediate apology and a rather incredible claim: "by thy beauties / I swear, I meant not disrespect to thee" (VIII, 233). His change of heart here and again under Alvarez's prodding is too sudden to be believable. Similarly, after he has imprisoned and later exiled Alphonzo, Rodriguez assumes that his love will make Ruzalla forget her father; however, when she vehemently rejects him, he quickly offers to pardon Alphonzo and make Ruzalla "rule her subject monarch." Nor is such vacillation made more credible by the remorse that the dying Rodriguez expresses over Ruzalla's corpse: "Thou fallen sweetness! 'twas my guilty love / Pointed thy father's dagger!—those pale lips / Cry, *Murder* on me!—hide me from that sight!—" (VIII, 286).

It is tempting to ascribe such ambiguity to inexperience and plain ineptitude in delineating psychological conflict. To an extent, this is probably true, particularly if we assume that Mackenzie wrote the original play in his late teens. However, a far more important factor stems from the fact that Mackenzie regards Rodriguez as little more than the agent who brings about the tragic events of the drama. As was the case with Appius, the author has no interest in developing the King's personality further than the demands of the plot require. He seems, in fact, uneasy about having to draw a "mixed character," preferring such clearly delineated representatives of good and evil as Lucius and Appulinius. It is also true that, if Mackenzie had fully developed Rodriguez's character and explored his inner conflict, his antagonist would have easily overshadowed the exemplary figure of Alphonzo. No doubt, this approach would have made for a more powerful tragedy within Aristotelian terms, but that was not Mackenzie's intention.

Like many of his contemporaries, Mackenzie conceived of tragedy almost exclusively in terms of pathos. To quote René Wellek, "The purgation of pity and fear was talked about, but interpreted not to mean purgation at all and not to refer to both pity *and* fear. Tragedy was increasingly considered simply a means of arousing pity."[12] Such tragedy is called "pathetic" by Lord Kames because its "ruling passion" is pity, whereas "moral tragedy" arouses not only our pity but our fears.[13] "A poem, whether dramatic or epic, that has nothing in view but to move the passions and to exhibit pictures of virtue and vice, may be distinguished by the name of *pathetic*: but where a story is purposely contrived to illustrate some moral truth, by showing that disorderly passions naturally lead to external misfortunes; such compositions may be denominated *moral.*"[14]

Because Mackenzie's purpose (as in *Virginia*) is clearly "to exhibit pictures of virtue and vice" rather than to "illustrate some moral truth," Rodriguez remains a shadowy, improbable character while attention is focused on the stern figure of Alphonzo. Tragedy is thus seen not dramatically but pictorially: it does not take shape around a conflict but around a character capable of evoking a strong and pleasing emotional response. In Mackenzie's preface, Alphonzo is described in terms of a tableau: "The character which most impressed itself on my imagination in writing this drama, was that of Alphonzo. In the enthusiasm natural to youth, I had conceived it standing on the high ground of heroic virtue and honour, fierce and implacable in vindication of those principles, yet open to that humanity and tender feeling, which I had perceived frequently to belong to minds of that description" (VIII, 205–06).

The plot becomes largely a means of emphasizing these traits in the hero—of filling in the portrait of "heroic virtue." Because the romantic young Mackenzie is too subjectively involved with his hero, there is no corrective, no voice of moderation to speak against Alphonzo's intemperate sense of honor. Only in retrospect did he come to recognize Alphonzo's glaring weaknesses; writing in 1802 to Dr. James Currie, he admits:

> The Tragedy of the *Spanish Father* I wrote, with great Rapidity, at a Time when I was not sufficiently aware of the difficulty of writing a Tragedy. There are, I think, (for I have not read it for a long time, & have now no Copy that is easily read) some good enough Strokes of high passion & of Tenderness in it; but probably Mr. Kemble was right in his Judgment that it was not well adapted for the Stage. I rather think, however, that the principal Character was well enough adapted to him; proud and passionate to excess, & rowzed to madness by Resentment for his Injuries, by outraged Honor, & by disapointed [*sic*] Tenderness, I recollect appropriating it at the Time to such an Actor as him, with a belief that that Character, at least, would *tell* (as the cant phrase is) in the Representation.[15]

At the time of composition, however, these excesses were justified and, if not openly admired, at least seen as inevitable in a person of Alphonzo's temperament and principles. His pride in the nobility and the virtue of his ancestors transcends all other considerations (VIII, 213). Thus it is not surprising to find him warning his daughter that he would be capable of sacrificing himself and her to redeem that heritage (VIII, 250–51).

To offset such severity and implacability, Alphonzo is endowed with those qualities that Mackenzie most values. He treats military prisoners with respect and humanity because "they are men too," and he has taught his subordinates "to reverence misfortune in the meanest." Like Virginius, he is capable of tenderness and sensitivity. Pedro recalls that, once before a battle when Alphonzo clasped his infant daughter, Ruzalla happened to be wrapped in a scarf that had been embroidered by her dead mother:

> Sudden you [Alphonzo] started back, and gave her to me,
> As if the sight had stung you; then, once more,
> To your big heaving bosom pressed the child,
> And wept and gazed, and gazed and wept again. (VIII, 262–63)

The incident is designed to make Alphonzo appear as a more sympathetic protagonist. In the context of the scene, however, it serves no dramatic purpose since Pedro's recollection in no way mitigates Alphonzo's anger against his daughter. Similarly, as he prepares to kill Ruzalla, he recollects her childhood innocence and how, after her mother's death, she became "the only joy of his declining age!" But such memories only tend to reawaken him to the magnitude of his loss:

> I had gathered in
> All my full hopes, and joyed to doat upon them;
> From the last battles of an honoured arm,
> Returned to rest, to happiness, and thee;
> To own myself a foolish fond old man,
> And pillow these white locks upon thy bosom!–
> This cuts the little thread of comfort left me,
> And blasts my age before the fall of nature!– (VIII, 284)

There is no real sense of conflict here, nor any evidence that Alphonzo is attempting to reassess his values—these are simply the words of an inflexible, self-pitying old man. The scene is designed to wring as much pity as possible from the audience before the impending catastrophe overtakes Alphonzo and his daughter. The trouble is, however, that our sympathy for Alphonzo's plight depends upon our accepting, or at least respecting, his inordinate sense of honor. We are much more likely to agree with Mackenzie's later assessment of his hero as "proud and passionate to excess" and to reserve our pity for his daughter.

Ruzalla is, in fact, the real tragic figure in this drama, though Mackenzie, fascinated by the stern virtue of Alphonzo's character, chose to relegate her to a subordinate position. Her personality, like that of Rodriguez, is never adequately developed, nor is her psychological conflict properly explored. Though, as the daughter of Alphonzo, she must be aware of the danger involved in dishonoring him, she nevertheless yields to Rodriguez's passionate advances without qualms or forebodings, claiming that after their first encounter, her "fancy kept behind / A too seducing image of Rodriguez" (VIII, 227). Physically attracted and vain of the idea of being loved by the King, she becomes an easy victim of her emotions.

All these facts are reported in retrospect in the familiar idiom of the eighteenth-century seduction novel. The action of the play begins a week later and finds Ruzalla a remorse-stricken, passive heroine, whom it is hard to envision as having been a thoughtless, romantically inclined young girl. Again, Mackenzie is more concerned with evoking a poignant mood of pathos than in delineating the psychological process that gave rise to such a state of mind. Like Virginia, Ruzalla is "in love with grief" and occupies her time in pensive solitude. This gives occasion for one of those plaintive scenes that is characteristic of Mackenzie. Ruzalla, her maid recounts, has a favorite lily that has become the "companion of her sadness":

> "And thou shalt die," I heard her say, "and shed
> Thy beauteous leaves; unspotted thou shalt shed them:
> When shall I fall like thee!" and then she raised
> Its bending head, and looked so very piteous,—
> Though it was but a flower, in sooth, I wept. (VIII, 245)

After Alphonzo knows the truth about his daughter, Ruzalla becomes a figure of despair and abject mortification vainly confronting her unrelenting father. Though he renounces her as his daughter and leaves her "to feel the pangs / Of infamy and guilt" (VIII, 269), she nevertheless prays to heaven to console and bless him. Convinced of the enormity of her crime, she believes it vain to plead for forgiveness, though she is hopeful that her father will some day show more leniency toward her memory. As she tells her friend, Elvira,

> Perhaps, when the dark grave has covered me,
> And every tongue is silent of my shame,
> He then may hear thee tell him of his child,
> Recal the memory of our better days,
> When she was innocent, and he was happy;
> Then if a soft forgiving tear he sheds,
> Tell him I hoped for that, and died contented. (VIII, 274–75)

Her attitude is calculated to arouse the audience's pity if not its tears. Indeed, the spectacle of a remorseful daughter demeaning and mortifying herself before an implacable but noble-minded father was likely to succeed as a rhetorical vehicle.

Such a scene was, moreover, particularly suited to Mackenzie's poetic talents. The simplicity of the blank verse aptly expresses Ruzalla's mood of quiet resignation. Equally effective is the lyrical quality of some lines: "Thou, my Ruzalla, art the single ray / That gilds the evening of thy father's age" (VIII, 222). But such artistic control is absent from the more passionate scenes where Mackenzie's diction becomes self-consciously elevated and theatrical, failing to convey the speaker's natural state of mind:

> Yes, my throbbing heart
> Has kept the dark opprobrious story down,
> And struggled with its pangs; but, ere my fate
> Shall pluck it thence,—for, oh! my boding soul
> Foresees detection blaze its light upon me . . . (VIII, 224)

All too frequently, Mackenzie's verse proves ineffective because he attempts to depict a character's emotions through clichés and derivative lines:

> Insult thee! Thou hast little known, Ruzalla,
> The power thou bear'st within this throbbing bosom.
> Look on me still with that transporting tenderness,
> As once within Montverdo's peaceful groves,– (VIII, 278)

Such passages help to foster the impression that Mackenzie's characters are lifeless puppets who are moved about self-consciously to create an emotional effect rather than a sense of reality. They lack an inner logic or continuity because they have been shaped and formulated artificially from the prototypes of an earlier theatrical tradition. It is no accident that Mackenzie's echoes of Shakespeare usually become unintentional parody. When Ruzalla, for example, reproaches Rodriguez for exiling her father, she reminds us of Cordelia:

> Alone, amidst the horrors of the night,
> Where does he wander?–Hark! the wind is up,
> And howls along the heath!–Must he lay down
> Upon the cold damp earth these hoary locks?– (VIII, 276)

But the comparison becomes ludicrous once we recognize its basic incongruity. When Shakespeare's Cordelia gazes on her father's sleeping countenance to ask, "Was this a face / To be oppos'd against the warring winds?," it is not so much to arouse the audience's pity as to articulate feelings that King Lear's tragic situation has already called forth. Ruzalla's words, on the other hand, are a contrived effort to evoke pathos where the events do not justify such a response. Similarly, when Alphonzo repeats Lear's words, "To own myself a foolish fond old man," they lack the sincerity and significance of the original and represent simply another random effort to inspire sympathy where no such reaction is warranted. This lack of correspondence between emotions and events accounts for the sentimentality of Mackenzie's tragedies.

III The Prince of Tunis

On March 1, 1773, Mackenzie announced to his cousin: "Your old friend The Prince of Tunis . . . is now in a fair way of stepping forth to the View of the Public."[16] Written "several years before,"[17] the play opened on March 8 at the Theatre Royal in Edinburgh and ran for five nights to crowded houses, plus a benefit performance on March 17.[18] The celebrated Mrs. Yates agreed to play the role of Zulima; and, according to Mackenzie's enthusiastic report, she revised the tragedy "with the most scrupulous Exactness, & suggested several Amendments equally convincing of Knowledge in theatrical Business & of critical Taste."[19] After her performance, however, his praise was more qualified: "She did not conceive the Character in quite so soft a Stile as I, &, I believe, most of my Friends who had read it, imagined. She took it up entirely on the great Line; & that Expression of Despair & Horror which at some Passages, She gave it, was inimitable."[20]

In the play, Arassid, Prince of Tunis, fearful of growing rebellion, goes to seek the aid of the Turkish Sultan. Barbarossa, sent by the Sultan to put down the revolt, becomes the Tunisian ruler by reporting that Arassid has died from a pestilence when he has actually had Arassid killed, or so he believes. Zulima, who has grown up with Arassid and been betrothed to him, is wooed by Barbarossa until finally she assents reluctantly; and the play opens on their wedding day, three months after Barbarossa's victory. Zeyda, Arassid's sister, brings Zulima news of a slave who claims that Arassid is alive but is imprisoned by the Sultan. Later Heli, Barbarossa's officer but a former friend of Arassid, claims that the prince was murdered at the bidding of Hassan, Barbarossa's evil lieutenant.

Hassan, meanwhile, gains proof that Heli has leagued himself with the rebellious leaders of Tunis and begins to plot Heli's death. The latter learns that Zulima is actually the daughter he thought lost at sea, while an emissary from the Sultan turns out to be Arassid, who has eluded and outwitted his enemies and now reveals himself to Zulima. Heli and his allies rebel and are victorious—Hassan is killed, and Barbarossa flees. However, Heli's reunion with his daughter is short-lived, for Barbarossa, out of feigned friendship, has given him to drink the wedding potion that Zulima, unknown to her husband, had previously poisoned to avenge Arassid's supposed murder. Torn by her sense of guilt at having unwittingly killed her father, Zulima stabs herself to death as news arrives that Turkish troops have landed and restored Barbarossa to power. Arassid rushes headlong into battle and dies though Barbarossa tries to save him. The play ends with a remorseful Barbarossa raving in madness.

The Prince of Tunis is founded upon an incident in William Robertson's *History of the Reign of the Emperor Charles V* (1769)[21] in which Alrachid actually flees from his tyrannical younger brother, Muley-Hascen, to implore the help of Barbarossa, ruler of Algiers. The treacherous Barbarossa arranges for Alrachid to be imprisoned in Constantinople: "he was arrested by order of the sultan, shut up in the seraglio, and was never heard of more."[22] Barbarossa then wins Tunis by pretending to come in Alrachid's name, who he claims lies sick in his ship. The people revolt against Muley-Hascen only to discover Barbarossa's subterfuge too late to make any effective resistance.

Such was the basis for Mackenzie's historical drama. Written in blank verse, *The Prince of Tunis* once again shows Mackenzie's strengths and weaknesses as a dramatic poet. His expository and descriptive passages are well executed and show considerable narrative skill:

> Suladdin says, that when his watch was changed,
> As, by the setting sun, he marked the sea,
> Dim on its level line he saw arise
> Objects that seemed a fleet, and grew upon him,
> Till darkness shut them out. (VIII, 169)

Mackenzie's limitations are revealed when the action is dramatized rather than reported, for he does not know how to delineate inner conflict naturally. When Hassan plays upon Barbarossa's fear of rebellion, the latter exclaims: "Thou distract'st my soul! / I am too young in virtue to withstand thee; / And yet I will" (VIII, 151). But his words are unconvincing because Barbarossa is describing and declaiming the conflict he should be experiencing dramatically.

As in *The Spanish Father,* emotional scenes are elevated through a self-conscious use of poetic diction:

> My wife! my daughter! thou whose infant softness
> The bursting billows cradled! call'st thou hence,
> With beckoning smiles, from yonder fields of light,
> The hoary, desolate, and friendless Heli?– (VIII, 176)

At other times, the language is heightened through alliteration and heroic imagery:

> My brother's blood,
> Whose body, blackened in the burning sun,
> The desart eagles fed on, cries revenge;
> And, like the lion from his tufted den,
> Awakes the sleeping fury of my soul. (VIII, 145)

Such passages show the influence not only of Restoration and Augustan tragedy but of Mackenzie's own poetic theory. Commenting upon modern poetry in terms that seem equally applicable to verse drama, he observes: "It will be admitted that everything that is natural is not poetry, of which the very essence seems to be a certain elevation and elegance of language above the standard of ordinary life. Nobleness and dignity are the attributes of poetry. These may belong to the feelings and sentiments of inferior persons, but the language in which those feelings and sentiments are to be conveyed seems to require a certain degree of elegance and elevation if it is to be entitled to the denomination of poetry."[23] It is this striving for "elegance and elevation" that accounts for much of Mackenzie's stilted blank verse and serves to mar his tragedies.

If *The Prince of Tunis* resembles *The Spanish Father* in its poetic style, it likewise shows similarities in its mode of characterization. We again have a weak figure of authority who is manipulated by a callous villain of principle, as well as a noble-minded soldier-father and his tragically doomed daughter. In spite of such similarities, however, *The Prince of Tunis* is a far more ambitious work than the earlier Mackenzie tragedies. Its characters possess greater complexity, though Mackenzie fails to realize their dramatic potentialities.

We see this difference most clearly by comparing the two extreme representatives of good and evil—Heli and Hassan. Heli is a mellowed Virginius or Alphonzo—tenderer, less stern, but still high-principled and idealistic: "I boast a heart, / The friend of justice and humanity" (VIII, 142). Not aware through most of the play that Zulima is his daughter, he is simply a long-suffering old man whose only remaining happiness is "conscious virtue." When he does discover Zulima's true identity, the nature of his response attests to his sensibility: "My wounded heart would lean upon her love, / Seek its lost peace, with big luxurious throbbings / Forget its woes, and wonder at its bliss" (VIII, 179).

In contrast, Hassan is the callous villain of principle whom Heli describes as incapable of being moved by pity. Like Appulinius and Alvarez, Hassan instinctively distrusts native goodness. Yet, while Appulinius and Alvarez are merely selfishly scheming villains, Hassan is a much more complex character. Though his influence upon Barbarossa is sinister, he remains completely loyal to him. His depravity is not motivated by simple egotism but by a consistently adhered-to cynicism that stems from "long-experienced falsehood." Unable to believe in the reality of disinterested virtue, he seeks ulterior motives to explain away its existence. Thus, when he finds proof that Heli is allied to the rebellious factions of Tunis, he rejoices because his own misanthropic view of mankind seems to him once more confirmed:

> Why, this is man;
> And Hassan knows him. With the sounds of fame,
> Of right, of freedom, talking like a god,
> He hides the baseness of a rotten heart. (VIII, 168)

Hassan, however, has misinterpreted Heli's character. As a man of virtue and sensibility, he is incapable of such duplicity. Lacking Hassan's cold pragmatism, he finds it hard to act because he is torn between loyalty to his prince and his vow to avenge Arassid's murder. Recognizing that the ends do not justify the means, that "muffled treason / Is not of virtue's colour," he nevertheless feels compelled to support justice, although Zeyda's argument that "Treason to him [Barbarossa] is virtue" does little to alleviate his misgivings:

> To the sons
> Of blind ambition, such distinctions heal
> The wounds of conscience; mine can feel it here
> Beneath their cover: Barbarossa trusts me. (VIII, 175)

Though the news that Hassan suspects him of treason finally spurs Heli to action, the implication, one Mackenzie later explores in his essay on Hamlet, is that sensibility can undermine resolution with the pale cast of thought.

Hassan, of course, is too pragmatic and callous to suffer from such doubts. He calls Barbarossa's growing qualms "that foolish weakness, / That baby conscience, that unsinews valour" (VIII, 148). Like Sindall, moreover, he has that "pliancy of disposition," which enables him to hide his true feelings. Characteristically, like all of Mackenzie's "Men of Feeling," Heli lacks such flexibility and hence gives himself away when Hassan tests him by mentioning Arassid's death:

> The workings of his soul denied him speech;
> His blood made fiery courses on his cheeks,
> And to the heavens he cast a furious look,
> As if he would have borrowed lightning thence
> To blast me with his eye; then turned, and left me,
> To hide his passion. (VIII, 148–49)

Between these representations of good and evil stands the figure of Barbarossa, another weak-minded, impetuous ruler. But, whereas Rodriguez's vacillations show little moral recognition or even consistency, Barbarossa's conscience is supposedly awakend by his love for Zulima: "since I saw her, / I have been taught to hate my former self, / In loving her" (VIII, 150). A similar testimony is given by Zeyda, Arassid's sister, who, unaware of her brother's supposed murder, is moved to sympathy by Barbarossa's show of emotions:

> But now he clasped my hand,
> A tear bedewed his cheek! "Zeyda," he said,
> "Perhaps I am unworthy of her love;
> Perhaps I have been—but—" he stopped, and heaved
> A sigh so piteous, that my heart forgot
> My father's sceptre, and was quite his friend. (VIII, 153)

Though Zeyda's reliability cannot be questioned, yet it is difficult to imagine Barbarossa in the role of the diffident, lovesick suitor. It must likewise be asked at what point his actions become sincere. When Zulima first meets him, he pretends to have been Arassid's friend; and he wins her favor by "mingling his tears / In one sad stream with" hers (VIII, 124). This of course is good strategy and has helped him to usurp the throne of Tunis. It is also one of the rare occasions in Mackenzie's works in which the testimony of the tear ducts can be questioned, unless we assume that his tears are an expression of remorse rather than an artifice of expediency.

Such ambiguity stems partly from the fact that we obtain so few internal glimpses of Barbarossa's character. He has only one brief soliloquy, and he lacks in Hassan the kind of confidant who would be sympathetic to his sense of guilt and remorse. The insights we do get are feeble attempts to suggest depth and consistency by means of Mackenzie's self-conscious borrowings from Shakespeare. Like Macbeth, he suffers from hallucinations about his victim, imagining that Arassid is calling him (VIII, 129). At another time, he takes a Claudius-like stance to picture himself as a guilt-ridden prisoner of his own conscience: "Still in my cup this spotted adder lies, / Taints every draught, that Fortune can bestow, / Unsceptres royalty, and blasts enjoyment!" (VIII, 134). But, unlike Claudius, he lacks the intellectual courage to recognize the futility of repenting for an act from which he still reaps the benefits. However, since for Mackenzie moral regeneration is largely a state of mind rather than the effect of a rational decision, we are expected to believe Barbarossa's simple claim: "I am changed / From what I have been" (VIII, 149).

These weaknesses in characterization reflect all too clearly Mackenzie's overriding design: the antagonist, as in *The Spanish Father,* is viewed primarily as an agent whose actions initiate the tragic consequences to follow. Barbarossa hardly appears in the last two acts because all effort is now directed toward wringing as much pathos as possible from the events that overwhelm Zulima and her father. Likewise, Barbarossa's seeming complexity and unrealized tragic potentiality stem from Mackenzie's effort to make the figure of Barbarossa (a pirate and ruthless tyrant in Robertson's *History*) sufficiently sympathetic to justify Zulima's accepting him. Though hers is not an infatuation, as was the case with Ruzalla, she does admit that "in some hour of weakness you [Barbarossa] o'ercame me" (VIII, 127). Hence it is not surprising that Mackenzie's means of making his character more sympathetic follows the pattern already utilized in *The Spanish Father*: Hassan's evil influence mitigates his master's moral responsibility, while the latter's increasing sense of remorse tends to arouse our sympathy. Yet such efforts lack consistency and credibility because Mackenzie could not allow Barbarossa's self-conflict to develop dramatically without overshadowing Zulima's pitiful fate, thereby converting an essentially "pathetic tragedy" into a "moral tragedy."

In many respects, Zulima's situation anticipates that of Julia de Roubigné. Zulima grows up with Arassid and, like Julia and Savillon, "each was like a twin-tuned lute." Whereas Julia's acceptance of Montauban depends upon the mistaken belief that Savillon is married, Zulima's acceptance of Barbarossa rests upon the erroneous assumption that Arassid is dead; and both face a tragic dilemma when their suppositions turn out to have been illusory. Likewise, each is pursued by a shrewd and pertinacious suitor. Barbarossa, like Montauban, plays upon the heroine's emotions to gain his end. Pretending to mourn Arassid as a dead friend, he earns her gratitude and finally her commiseration: "He wooed me in compassion's gentle form, / To chase despair and anguish from his breast" (VIII, 124). Reluctantly, she at last assents to his "ceaseless importunity," but his victory is as empty as Montauban's since he gains "the promise, not the will."

Such resemblances between plots do not, however, extend to the depth of realism of the two works: the psychological analysis and relentless introspection that impress us in *Julia de Roubigné* are scarcely to be found in *The Prince of Tunis*. As with Barbarossa, Mackenzie's view of his heroine is external—he never probes her character nor sees her as an integral personality. When Zulima learns that the man she has just married instigated the supposed death of her lover, her response is artificial and highly derivative as she rapidly changes from a passive mourner into a resolute agent of vengeance:

> Soft, I would breathe a moment!—Barbarossa!
> My curses blast him!—Is he not my husband?
> The murderer of my love!—See how he glares,
> And points his wounds; whose purple mouths unfold
> Their lips afresh, and cry aloud for vengeance!—
> Hast thou no dagger for a hand resolved? (VIII, 158)

As in his earlier tragedies, we have the impression that Mackenzie creates situations not so much to beset his characters with inner conflicts as to evoke feelings and moods from their reactions. Retrospecting about this tragedy in old age, he comments revealingly: "The play, it must be confessed, has many faults, particularly in the winding up of the plot; but it has some good poetry, and passages in which there was room for Mrs. Yates's powers of passionate declamation to exert themselves."[24] Zulima's soliloquy, at the beginning of Act IV, certainly offered such an opportunity. When sending the poisoned wedding drink to Barbarossa, she invokes supernatural spirits in the manner of a Lady Macbeth:

> Ye ministers of vengeance! Ye who ride
> On tempests' wings, and point the lightnings' spear!
> Who split the bosom of the trembling earth!
> Or from the phials of offended Heaven
> Pour its black venom on the deathful gale!
> Inspire my soul with unrelenting rage,
> And chase the busy fears, that rise upon me! (VIII, 184–85)

Yet if such a speech suited Mrs. Yates's histrionic talents, she was for Mackenzie (as mentioned before) less satisfactory in those soft scenes of melancholy that were his forte. Until the third act, Zulima is one of those mournful, resigned heroines (much like Ruzalla and Virginia) that appeal to his fondness for pathos:

> I am in love with sorrows. I could sit
> The live-long day, and ruminate upon them.
> Methinks there is a dignity in sorrow,
> Lord of its sighs, and conqueror of the world! (VIII, 135)

It is, however, the last act that best reveals Mackenzie's rhetorical method. The denouement confronts his heroine with a series of revelations calculated to elicit a wide range of emotions. And, characteristically, events act on her rather than offer her a choice of action, each carrying with it its own inevitability that makes her its passive and ironic victim. The discovery that Arassid lives creates a hopeless dilemma for her since she has just married his would-be murderer: "I am not what I was: the serpent's touch / Has turned this flower to poison" (VIII, 189). But the despair of this situation is quickly dwarfed by the horror of succeeding events: the discovery that Heli is her father is followed almost immediately by the realization that she has unwittingly brought about his death. Such a climax offered Mackenzie the kind of crescendo of pathos that he later felt ill at ease about. The dying Heli blesses his daughter and prays to God to forgive her. Zulima, guilt-stricken and growing mad, calls heaven's vengeance upon herself before she commits suicide:

> No: let me curse; and, if the thunder sleeps,
> Awake its hottest bolt, and call it here!—
> I am not mad; I know I am not mad!
> This old man was my father!—Murdered! murdered!
> [*Throwing herself on the Body of her Father.*] (VIII, 196)

Her remorse is calculated to evoke in us the strongest sense of pity since she bears little responsibility for the chain of events that have turned her into an unwitting parricide. Though Heli's death is the indirect result of her attempt to poison her husband, the fact that Barbarossa has usurped the Tunisian throne and murdered the rightful ruler (or so she believes) who is also her lover largely exonerates her and gives her death that aura of pathos which dominates all of Mackenzie's tragedies.

IV False Shame

Mackenzie's only comedy, based on *La Fausse Inconstance; ou, Le Triomphe de l'Honnêteté* (1787) by Fanny de Beauharnais,[25] deals with a young man's fear of ridicule and its consequences. Sedley, having been brought up in the country, goes to London to taste fashionable life after coming into an estate of seven thousand pounds a year. His cousin, Sir Charles Dormer, plays upon his fear in order to introduce him to a life of deceit and intrigue. Mountfort, Sedley's former tutor who is believed to have died in India, returns to England in the disguise of one Captain Wilkins, a supposed friend of the "deceased." He witnesses the seeming corruption of his former pupil, whom he had appointed guardian to his daughter Julia; and he decides to remove her from Sedley's influence. Since Wilkins claims to be Julia's co-guardian, Sir Charles, who is enamored of the girl, has Miss Danby, his accomplice, try to bribe him into giving up his guardianship. However, to protect Sir Charles, Miss Danby pretends to be speaking for Sedley. Wilkins is incensed by the offer, and Miss Danby persuades Sir Charles that their best stratagem now is to encourage the Captain's anger into a real quarrel with Sedley. Miss Danby will meanwhile entice Julia to her house, where Sir Charles will be able to seduce her.

Ignorant of this arrangement, Lady Dormer has made an assignation with Sedley at Miss Danby's house. She arrives and hides her face behind a mask when her husband appears. Sir Charles, believing her to be Julia, tries to make love to her but is interrupted by the arrival of Wilkins, who finally unmasks Lady Dormer. Sedley now arrives with his old servant William who, never having been deceived by Mountfort's disguise, gives away Wilkins's true identity and reports that Sedley has rescued Julia from Miss Danby's clutches. Mountfort and Sedley are reconciled, and Sedley promises never to play the "White Hypocrite" again and receives the hand of Julia from her forgiving father.

Originally called *The Force of Fashion,* the play was performed at Covent Garden for one night only on December 5, 1789. In the preface to the published version, called *False Shame, or The White Hypocrite* and included in his collected *Works,* Mackenzie speculates about the reason for its failure:

> This Comedy was unsuccessful in the representation; and, in truth, it is not, I believe, well calculated for the stage. It suffered, perhaps, a little by my absence from London, and the secresy which I thought it prudent to hold with regard to its author. Mr. Harris shewed every attention to it, and entertained the most sanguine assurance of its success; yet I have been told by some theatrical people, that (owing probably to the state of Covent Garden theatre at the time) it was ill cast, as the playhouse phrase is, and the principal part (that of *Mountfort*) very indifferently played.[26] That character is of a kind difficult to play; depending on feelings sometimes altogether suppressed, and often, when expressed in words, expressed in that short and stifled manner, which, in my idea, suited the situation and feelings of the speaker; its representation rather required aid from the performer, than lent it him in the performance. (VIII, 291)

"The general idea of the piece," he admits, "is imperfectly brought out," and then he adds: "I had once thoughts of remodelling the piece, and of trying to place some of the characters in more theatrical situations; but I gave up the attempt, afraid of an alteration which might again expose me to a failure which I had once experienced. So I give the comedy here as it originally stood" (VIII, 292).

The fact is, however, that Mackenzie did make changes some time between the play's performance and its publication nineteen years later. When we compare the original manuscript of *The Force of Fashion* submitted to the Lord Chamberlain[27] with the printed version of *False Shame,* a good number of alterations are apparent. Many of these are merely stylistic changes, but some indicate a definite shift in characterization. Together with the change of title, Mackenzie provided a new epilogue, probably because the first one specifically refers to the old title. The first epilogue is, moreover, merely a humdrum recital of the "despotic Sway" of that idol Fashion, while the second is a witty argument by Lady Dormer to the effect that "*Hypocrisy's* a very useful thing."[28] There are also many cuts and revisions in the manuscript (probably to make it conform to the acted version), most of which Mackenzie ignored in preparing the play for publication. The longest of these excisions removes from the manuscript all of the satirical action involving a ludicrous group of virtuosos, a scene comprising almost half of the first act. In *False Shame*, a fair part of this scene remains, preserving one of the dilettantes, the antiquarian Dr. Mummy, though Mackenzie eliminated all the dialogue involving Mr. Petal, Mr. Distich, Dr. Phlogiston, and Mr. Speculum. From these deleted passages, however, we get a clue to the date of composition of the play. On the first numbered leaf of the manuscript, as elsewhere, there are references to the *World, or Fashionable Advertiser*, a London daily newspaper that did not begin publication until 1787.[29] It was on January 6 of that year, moreover, that the *Lounger* ceased publication, probably providing Mackenzie with the leisure to make another attempt to win acceptance on the London stage.

Although the machinations of Sir Charles and Miss Danby are never allowed to prosper far enough to bring serious harm to the good characters, the basic format is reminiscent of Mackenzie's tragedies. Mountfort is another variation of the noble soldier-father striving to protect his daughter, while Julia possesses that characteristic pensive quality which we have seen in most of Mackenzie's heroines. Similarly, Sir Charles Dormer is one more villain of passion, whereas Miss Danby typifies the villain of principle. It is only in the temporary aberration of Sedley that a new dramatic course is explored.

Yet here too correspondences are to be found if we turn back to Mackenzie's fiction. Ned Sedley appears briefly in *The Man of Feeling* in the fragment called "The Pupil." As an old man, he recounts for Harley how his tutor Mountford managed to protect him from the corrupting influence of Respino. Though *Mountford* becomes *Mountfort* in *False Shame* (the manuscript of *The Force of Fashion* still preserves the original spelling), there can be little doubt of Mackenzie's borrowings from his first novel. Indeed, Sedley, in *False Shame* recounts: "When a boy, I was placed under his [Mountfort's] care; a kind of tutor, sir; I was indebted to him for a great deal of good learning, which now it will cost me nearly as much time to forget" (VIII, 324).

We noted earlier in reference to Billy Annesly that his debasement was almost inevitable because he lacked a Mountford to offset Sindall's concerted effort to corrupt him. Sedley, in spite of Mountfort's former tutelage, is in a similar position when he comes under the influence of Sir Charles. He is, in fact, all the more vulnerable because of his inordinate fear of ridicule. Yet Sedley shows no signs of possessing this weakness in "The Pupil." On the contrary, his final rejection of Respino reveals a degree of self-confidence that he obviously lacks in *False Shame*: "You [Respino] may possibly be merry with your companions at my weakness, as I suppose you will term it. I give you leave for derision: you may affect a triumph; I shall feel it" (I, 228).

Mackenzie changed Sedley's character because he wanted to portray in his comedy "a young man, of the most virtuous dispositions and amiable feelings, overpowered by a false shame, and led into conduct unworthy of him" (VIII, 292). This theme, as we have seen, he had only recently examined in the "Story of Father Nicholas." Though Sedley shares St. Hubert's "extreme sensibility of shame," he is able to escape the latter's fate largely because of Mackenzie's comic approach to the theme. Yet the tragic potentialities remain and find expression in Mountfort's last speech: "He who is first such a hypocrite from vanity, or from fear, will be in danger of becoming, in truth, the character he personates" (VIII, 427).

"A "Man of Feeling" is particularly apt to face such a temptation since his acute sensibility and imagination, as we have observed, make him naturally self-conscious and hence sensitive to the way others respond to him. Harley's moral strength is derived in large part from his refusal to permit the ridicule of a callous world to affect his ideal mode of conduct. Yet even he, we must remember, cannot completely ignore the persistent voice of the "man without." However, whereas Harley will not accommodate himself to the demands of a corrupt society, though ill at ease in the knowledge of its disdain, Sedley has begun to compromise his principles although he has not yet, like St. Hubert, learned to blunt his "natural feelings of rectitude":

Sir Char. The world is full of rogues and fools; a wise man must accommodate himself to both.
Sed. That accommodation I find it difficult to reconcile myself to; yet often, from a silly sort of shame, I submit to it, till a better sort of shame takes me to task for having done so. (VIII, 311)

Sedley's corruption, then, is largely a façade behind which he tries to hide his native goodness from the jeers of a cynical world. When he helps free an officer on half-pay from debtor's prison, he pretends to his valet to be seducing the man's wife. Only when egged on by Sir Charles, who plays upon his fears of ridicule, does he attempt to assume the role his nature abhors. But his resolution to take advantage of Julia's helpless position falters as soon as he catches sight of her: "no sooner had she spoken, had she looked when she spoke, had she smiled . . . than I melted down again to a fond respectful—fool, you [Sir Charles] would call it" (VIII, 361).

Though "but a sorry player," as he himself admits later, Sedley nevertheless succeeds in misleading Wilkins because he is determined to convince the latter that he is "not the vulgar, sober, whining thing he may have been taught by Mountfort to imagine" (VIII, 322). Sedley's masquerade must of course work to fulfill the demands of the plot. At times, however, his emotions master him in his meeting with Wilkins since Mackenzie wanted his hero's inner conflict to become transparent to the audience. The manuscript carries elaborate stage directions for that purpose: "Sedley looks at him [Wilkins] at first with a Complacency, which he afterwards checks with an affected Indifference & Haughtiness of Air. During their whole Conversation, Sedley must wear a Look of Embarrassment, struggling to keep down his natural Feelings under this Mask of assumed Indifference. He must often shew in his Countenance Feelings ready to overpower him, while his Tongue & an affected Negligence of Manner awkwardly contradict it."[30]

The situation is naturally comical, but for Mackenzie it also offered a solution to a problem he had never actually solved in his tragedies. The moral ambiguity that mars the characterization of both Rodriguez and Barbarossa is avoided in the portrayal of Sedley because, as a mock villain, he does not bring into question the ethical nature of Julia's love for him. His inner conflicts, his sense of embarrassment and shame, are convincing because they are the natural result of his particular dilemma rather than merely the means of superimposing a more sympathetic overlay on his character. Instead of vacillating between good and evil with little consistency or credibility, as is the case with Rodriguez and Barbarossa, Sedley's moral regeneration follows a convincing psychological pattern. The awkwardness and uneasiness with which he plays the fashionable libertine prepare us for his final reformation. Though he has a short-lived resolution before his meeting with Wilkins to be "a coward thus no longer," his true change of heart comes only when he recognizes the real price he will have to pay for his fear of ridicule. Revolted by Sir Charles's exhortations to challenge Wilkins and make love to his friend's wife (who happens, unknown to Sir Charles, to be Lady Dormer), Sedley finally begins to question the legitimacy of fashion's rule: "What is this fashion, that I should obey it at such expence? and whence is that superiority, that entitles it to laugh at me?" (VIII, 408).

Significantly, moral change is now conveyed by means of argument and action rather than by falling back on the stale idiom of sensibility. By rejecting Lady Dormer's amorous advances and by resolving to fire into the air in the ensuing duel with Wilkins, Sedley demonstrates his goodness and his newly acquired self-confidence in the face of a jeering, callous world. He fulfills, moreover, the demands made earlier by Wilkins when, unimpressed by Sedley's munificence (he has secretly sent Julia money), he had defined true generosity: "It is not parting with money, which the habits of extravagance have taught them to undervalue, that entitles such men to be called humane or generous. Let them forego one favourite indulgence for the sake of humanity; let them sacrifice one selfish passion to the good of others, and then tell us of their benevolence and generosity" (VIII, 397). Since his words are in part a close paraphrase of a passage in *Mirror*, No. 23, that condemns Charles Surface as a "profligate hero," it is quite likely that Mackenzie chose this opportunity to restate allusively his criticism of Richard Brinsley Sheridan's hero in *The School for Scandal.*

The didactic value of Sedley's moral education is, of course, evident: it gives Mackenzie an opportunity to expose the folly of conforming to a degenerate society. At the heart of that corruption lies a fashionable nonchalance and an insensitivity that Mackenzie, like so many of his contemporaries,[31] attributed to the influence of Lord Chesterfield's *Letters to his Son* (1774):

> In the intercourse of ordinary life, the late founder of a school of politeness recommended a certain indifference or *nonchalance* of manner, as the characteristic of a well-bred man. The system has since his time flourished and prevailed in a most extensive degree, and, like all other systems that war on nature, has been carried a good deal further by the disciples, than it is probable their masters intended, "Nous avons changé tout cela," says the Mock Doctor of Moliere, when his patient's father ventured to suppose that the heart lay on the left side of the body. The fine gentleman of Lord Chesterfield has made a change still greater; the heart is struck out of his anatomy altogether.[32]

Wilkins, after seeing Sedley, is convinced that his former pupil has already adopted this mode of conduct. Sedley, he tells Julia, is "depraved not by passion, but on system; that despicable, selfish, unfeeling system, in which modern refinement has taught her votaries to triumph. I can make allowance for the wanderings of youth, when levity misleads, or passion impels it; but this cold apathy of vice so chills, so petrifies the heart, that neither returning honour can warm, nor awakened conscience rouse it" (VIII, 335). This distinction is one we have seen run through much of Mackenzie's works: man can be corrupted either by losing control over his emotions or by learning to control them too well. The one becomes a villain of passion; the other ends up as villain of principle. The latter case offers, however, the greatest danger, since moral regeneration is largely an emotional experience toward which such a man has deliberately deadened his senses, while the villain of passion by his very nature retains the capacity for regeneration.

Sir Charles, though driven by his infatuation for Julia into a series of unscrupulous acts, yet has qualms about instigating a quarrel between Sedley and Wilkins and is moved by the tears of a loyal servant. When old William assures him that he would lay down his life for Sedley, Sir Charles momentarily senses his own corruption: "How this old man loves his master! The tears were on his cheek, and he spoke so from the warmth of his heart, that mine, callous as it is to such foolery, was smitten, and could scarcely play the hypocrite to him. After all, there is something in this same virtue, that one can't help feeling now and then in spite of one. Not all the gold I can bribe my rascals with, ever purchased from them one such tear as William's" (VIII, 402–03).

The situation is ironic because Sir Charles's emotional response contradicts his own mode of conduct. Contemptuous of morality and sensibility, he sees them only as a useful guise for taking advantage of those still innocent enough to admire such qualities. His hope is to seduce Julia by putting on "that old-fashioned cloak of virtue and feeling" which he had made his rival Sedley ashamed to wear. When he addresses her at Miss Danby's house (though he is, of course, really confronting the masked figure of his own wife), he tries to affect an air of sincerity by mouthing the ideals of sensibility: "Formed for the tenderest sympathies of friendship and of love, it has been my misfortune to be joined to one who is perfectly unsusceptible of either; . . . Nay, do not start at the declaration,—you must have seen, though I was careful to hide my attachment, you must have seen how much it possessed by heart. There are souls, which, by an instinctive sort of impulse, involuntarily attract one another" (VIII, 414).

Sir Charles could not, of course, be farther from the truth. He rejects all notions of love or compatibility in marriage, adhering to a cynically pragmatic view of one's wife: "A wife is a woman, who is to take a man's name, and may chance, during the first year or two, to bring an heir to his estate; to do sometimes the honours of his table (when the company is not too good for her;) and to let women, that might otherwise be scrupulous, come about his house. But as for his companion—I don't think I have exchanged a dozen sentences with Lady Dormer these three months" (VIII, 317). Needless to say, Mackenzie abhorred such values and was alarmed by their widespread acceptance. In an early letter to his cousin, he complains: "The romantic is now exploded in every Thing; in Marriage it is fallen in Proportion; and Matches of mere Conveniency are talk'd of at an age when the Youth of former Times used to be ignorant of the Word."[33]

Lady Dormer shares many of her husband's vices, and she too tries to justify herself by insisting that "one must accommodate to one's society," just as she also relies on the idiom of sensibility to achieve her objective—alluring Sedley. " 'Tis not with common-place souls," she assures him, "that mine can vibrate" (VIII, 365). Lady Dormer appears, nevertheless, far less reprehensible than her husband since his cynical infidelity confers upon her a certain pathos if not also some justification for her conduct. "Do you not pity me then," she asks Sedley, "married (as most women of my rank are) before I knew myself; wedded, not to a man, but to a settlement; a mere alliance of conveniency" (VIII, 364).

In revising his play, Mackenzie sought to emphasize these aspects of her character by expanding her soliloquy at the end of the second act. Originally, she voices her jealousy of Julia and makes plans to entice Sedley. In *False Shame,* a number of lines are added to her soliloquy in which she seeks to justify her conduct: "But is it quite right in me to draw his eyes that way? quite fair to Sir Charles my husband?—How the deuce now did that word contrive to come across my conscience? the word *wife,* I'll be sworn, never comes across Sir Charles's; and, as a married woman is fairly entitled to the attentions of *one* man, if her husband is not that one, may she not try to find such a one for herself?" (VIII, 351). At the same time, Mackenzie deleted several incriminating lines that call attention to Lady Dormer's duplicity in claiming to have Julia's best interest at heart when she is actually jealous of the attention the girl receives from Sedley and her husband. In *The Force of Fashion,* Lady Dormer assures Wilkins: "Sir you will always find me happy to receive you, & equally interested with yourself in the Welfare of Miss Mountford." And then observes *solus* in what originally had constituted the beginning of her soliloquy: "So—how much one can do with a little Hypocrisy at one's Heart, & a few fine Words on one's Tongue."[34] In *False Shame,* all these lines are eliminated.

Yet such instances of intrigue and double-dealing pale before the machinations of Miss Danby. Where Lady Dormer and even Sir Charles uneasily sense at times their own duplicity, no such qualms beset Miss Danby. As a true villain of principle, she possesses neither the emotional susceptibility nor the moral restraint that sometimes gets the better of Sir Charles. When she proposes to arrange a quarrel between Wilkins and Sedley, Sir Charles is hesitant though he admires Miss Danby's lack of scruples: "You women, Di, have no restraints on your inclinations, no qualms to come across you in the progress of them. Would not this be going a little too far, to make them cut one another's throats, to make way for me to the girl?" But Miss Danby, like other Mackenzie characters, such as Appulinius, Alvarez, and Hassan, knows how to manipulate her patron's emotions:

> *Miss Dan.* Your love, I find, is not half so sharp set as my resentment. But you think too deeply of the consequences; they shall but scramble on a point of honour, and give you an opportunity of running away with the prize in the mean time.
> *Sir Char.* Shall I indeed?—that dear, soft, artless, bewitching girl!—To obtain her, Danby, you shall make me all the rogue you would have me to be. 'Tis her fault to be so bewitching, eh?— (VIII, 379)

Sharing Sindall's "pliancy of disposition," she easily ingratiates herself with "honest William" by "speaking of the good old times at Sedley-Hall and making him presents of Thomas-a-Kempis, and the Whole Duty of Man, for Sunday's reading in the country" (VIII, 385). It is, however, by feigning the characteristics of sensibility that Miss Danby has achieved her greatest success. Having originally come to London as Dorothy Dobson "to be put apprentice to a little mantua-maker," she has improved her station and acquired "an elegant small house" by becoming Diana Danby, "poetess and sentimentalist" (one who speaks in sentiments like Joseph Surface). In reality, a pander who provides suitable accommodations for the affairs of both Sir Charles and Lady Dormer, she hides her role behind the effusive display of delicacy and benevolence that has become second nature to her. When Sir Charles urges her to be herself in his presence, she complains: "I can't immediately put off this cant, which I am obliged to use to the dupes of it. By the help of this high-flown style, I have got into the good graces of this same Wilkins, who seems to be as honourable and sentimental as the best of us" (VIII, 353). It is undoubtedly under her tutelage that Sir Charles has learned "this high-flown style." When she approaches Wilkins with Dormer's veiled proposal, she assures him that "there are souls with whom sympathy anticipates time, and connects us at first sight," a sentiment Sir Charles echoes when he imagines he is addressing Julia.

In *The Force of Fashion*, Miss Danby appears as merely an unscrupulous opportunist who schemes for the benefit of her patron. In *False Shame,* her character becomes more vicious through a revealing soliloquy added at the beginning of Act III. Apparently, Mackenzie felt that her odious act of trying to betray Julia into the clutches of Sir Charles needed more adequate motivation. She is, therefore, made to appear vindictive and contemptuous of Julia, loathing her for her moral superiority: "So, this girl takes it into her head to suspect me, and to lecture Lady Dormer on the subject. What is this virtue, that its owners should give themselves such airs! As things go now-a-days—and a girl with nothing too! This old-fashioned virtue, like an old-fashioned gown, may be worn by the rich if they please; but when it is the best of the wardrobe, 'twill be looked on as a cast-off thing, and valued accordingly. But I shall be even with her, if my invention and Sir Charles's courage fail not" (VIII, 352). Yet if Julia has become suspicious of Miss Danby, it seems implausible for her to believe the latter's claim of coming to fetch her in Wilkin's name.

Such a discrepancy is, however, unlikely to become noticeable because Julia Mountfort is a shadowy figure, one rarely seen directly although most of the plot revolves around her. In a play of one hundred thirty pages, she is present for only sixteen pages, having two meetings with Wilkins and then reappearing shortly before the play ends. In other respects, however, she is clearly reminiscent of Mackenzie's former heroines. Sedley describes Julia as "gentle, elegant—shaded by affliction, dignified by her sorrows!" And once again the mother is made to die in the heroine's infancy in order to enable Mackenzie to create more of those affecting scenes between a high-minded, widowed father and his submissive daughter. Whereas in *The Prince of Tunis* neither is aware of their kinship, in *False Shame* it is only the daughter that is ignorant, believing herself a forlorn orphan. The situation is obviously pathetic, and Mackenzie does not hesitate to exploit its emotional potential. At her first meeting with her disguised father, Julia instinctively senses his delicacy and goodness and determines to trust him implicitly: "I pass over the ceremonial of a first interview, and, judging of the nobleness of his [her father's] representative by what I have been proud to hear of him, I speak at once to the heart from the heart; from a poor, orphan, unfriended girl, to one who can feel—Pardon this freedom, Captain Wilkins—" (VIII, 330).

The fact that Julia is allowed on stage only in her meetings with Wilkins may be viewed as a flaw in the play. Sedley's meeting with her, when he is determined to flirt with Julia only to have his resolution overthrown as soon as she addresses him, is reported rather than dramatized although its comic potentiality is obvious. Possibly, however, this was the very reason for leaving the scene unwritten. Perhaps Mackenzie was unwilling to bring his pensive, idealized heroine in contact with the protagonists of his comic plot for fear of diminishing her credibility in the presence of more realistically executed characters.

As such, the absence of this scene indicates a characteristic problem of Sentimental comedy: its precarious union of purely comic elements with sententious and pathetic features. Yet Mackenzie in his prologue boasts of the hybrid nature of his play. After a debate between the rival sisters of Comedy, the "laughing Muse" and her sister "Sentiment," in which the traditional arguments against each school of comedy are recited, he announces a compromise solution:

> To-night our bard,—I praise his courage for't,—
> To either sister tries to pay his court;
> Some comic characters attempts to sketch,
> Some deeper feelings humbly hopes to reach.
> Your hearts, he knows, how quick soe'er to seize
> True comic mirth, those serious feelings please;
> The tear for worth, triumphant or oppressed,
> Drops through the sunshine of the gayest breast; (VIII, 294)

The truth is, however, that the play arouses few tears because "true comic mirth" obviously predominates. Not only are we rarely allowed to see Julia on stage, but we do not share Wilkins's disillusioned view of Sedley since we are able to discern his true worth behind the facade of libertinism. We can, therefore, enjoy his inept masquerade and discomfort without feeling serious anxiety about the outcome. As a result, *False Shame* largely succeeds as an amusing and effective comedy and is undoubtedly Mackenzie's best play.

Nor is it by mere chance that his one comedy is superior. Though Mackenzie has never gained recognition as a comic writer, it is that very quality, as we have said, that gives his *Man of Feeling* its unique tone and sense of detachment. Through his narrator, the novelist gained an objective perspective from which to view his hero. Similarly, it is the comic form itself that objectified Mackenzie's view as a playwright. Sensing the hazard of introducing a pensive heroine into comedy, particularly where a sham form of sensibility was to be exposed, he suppressed for once his love of pathos in order to submerge Julia as much as the plot permitted. Comedy, in a sense, liberated him from the narrow rhetorical confines that tragedy had assumed for him and enabled him to achieve a degree of realism and control his earlier plays had sorely lacked.

CHAPTER 7

Critical Essays

IN a period of six months from June 18, 1785 to January 14, 1786, Mackenzie published four papers on literary genres in the weekly issues of the *Lounger*. Two are devoted to tragedy and one each to the novel and to comedy. Since Mackenzie had himself worked earlier in the first two genres, we would expect his general estimate to be high, but nothing could be further from the truth. Each form in turn is condemned for its corrupting effect because Mackenzie approaches his subject not as a practicing writer but, as he admits himself, "in the hardihood of a moralist." Nor is this attitude surprising if we recognize the traditional role of the essay-critic.

To quote Robert D. Mayo, "by a long and venerable tradition . . . the periodical essayist was led to view his column as a kind of ethical tribunal, where his first duty, if not his only duty, was to the truths of reason and laws of principle. . . . more purely literary problems were laid aside in favor of the overwhelming question of the moral potentialities of works of fiction, particularly their effect upon the young and the inexperienced."[1] Mackenzie explored this question of effect by examining empirically the moral efficacy of literature. As such, much of his approach is psychological, and his conclusions often depart from generally accepted doctrine. They illuminate, like no other part of his writings, the disparity between the circumspect moralist and the idealized world of much of his drama and fiction.

Mackenzie wrote two other critical papers that for their intrinsic value far overshadow his genre essays. In each, he examines a Shakespearean character and attempts to find a ruling principle that reconciles the disparate elements of his personality. Following the lead of such contemporary Shakespearean critics as William Richardson, Maurice Morgann, and Thomas Whately, Mackenzie views both Hamlet and Falstaff as self-contained characters who possess an identity quite apart from the plays in which they appear. Largely silenced here is the fastidious moralist of the genre essays, and in his place is a keenly perceptive critic who anticipates in his intuitive grasp of Shakespeare some of the principles of Romantic criticism.

I *"On Novel-writing"*

Lounger, No. 20, "On Novel-writing,"[2] is the first of the genre essays, and parts of it are reminiscent of Johnson's *Rambler,* No. 4, on modern fiction, written thirty-five years earlier. Like his predecessor, Mackenzie sees the novel's audience as comprising "the young and the indolent." The "more respectable class of literary men" have nothing but contempt for the genre, but Mackenzie asks if such disdain is really warranted: "Considered in the abstract, as containing an interesting relation of events, illustrative of the manners and characters of mankind, it surely merits a higher station in the world of letters than is generally assigned to it." The novelist shares most of the problems faced by writers of epics and dramas, and he has need of a similar "degree of invention, judgment, taste, and feeling." Since he deals, moreover, with common life, he exposes himself (as Johnson had pointed out earlier) to everyone's judgment and cannot hide his faults behind "the pomp of poetry, nor the decoration of the stage."

So far Mackenzie seems to be striving to defend the novel, but he has been discussing fiction in the abstract. When he moves to a concrete consideration of the contemporary novel, his attitude shifts markedly. Ease of judging fiction has led many to assume that its composition would be equally effortless; as a result, the novel has been debased to the point where gifted writers have "retired from it in disgust, and left it in the hands of the unworthy." Its degradation is not, however, limited to technical inferiority but extends to its "moral or instructive purpose." His real object comes to light as he extends his charge of immorality to include the works of those "superior men" who emphasize the *dulce* over the *utile* and even some who had "intended to aid the cause of virtue."

Yet, lest he "carry the idea of the dangerous tendency of all novels quite so far as some rigid moralists have done," he turns once more to an abstract consideration of the form. As a didactic vehicle, the novel has a more "immediate tendency" than other genres to produce "a certain refinement of mind" because its subject matter closely approximates the reader's own world of experience. Johnson had made a similar point in order to emphasize that "the best examples only should be exhibited"; Mackenzie, however, goes much farther in examining the function of the novel. He conceives its role as particularly suited to the needs of an advanced society: "Those who object to them [novels] as inculcating precepts, and holding forth examples, of a refinement which virtue does not require, and which honesty is better without, do not perhaps sufficiently attend to the period of society which produces them. The code of morality must necessarily be enlarged in proportion to that state of manners to which cultivated aeras give birth."

But, if such is the purpose of the novel, it has been strangely perverted from its objective:

> The principal danger of novels, as forming a mistaken and pernicious system of morality, seems to me to arise from that contrast between one virtue or excellence and another, that war of duties which is to be found in many of them, particularly in that species called the sentimental. These have been chiefly borrowed from our neighbours the French, whose style of manners, and the very powers of whose language, give them a great advantage in the delineation of that nicety, that subtilty of feeling, those entanglements of delicacy, which are so much interwoven with the characters and conduct of the chief personages in many of their most celebrated novels.

Mackenzie's position is undoubtedly puzzling, if not paradoxical; for he seems to be indirectly condemning the kind of novel most qualified to broaden the "code of morality." Moreover, he appears by implication to be renouncing, as has often been pointed out,[3] his own works of fiction. The fact is, however, that Mackenzie attacks what he calls the "sentimental novel," not for its delineation and encouragement of sensibility, but for perverting that emotional susceptibility from its legitimate function—the cultivation of virtue. It is this "separation of conscience from feeling" that alarms him and elicits such a harsh reaction.

To understand Mackenzie's position, we must recall his beliefs and the challenges they faced in the closing decades of the century. The function of literature, indeed of all the fine arts, was to cultivate and increase our sensibility by making us more responsive to impressions: "I imagine," writes Mackenzie, that "being somewhat conversant with the fine Arts is one of the most powerful Improvements of the Mind. There is something of an acquired as well as a natural Delicacy, & the Soul as well as the Body has Nerves, which are only affected in a certain indescribable Manner, & gain by frequent Exertion a very superior Degree of Feeling."[4] Such "acquired Delicacy" must not, however, be viewed as an end in itself but as a means toward moral improvement. For Mackenzie, the value of Abraham Cowley's poetry, for example, stems from the fact that "there is a pensive tenderness in his poems that gives them a ready accordance with minds of sensibility, and leads to the feeling and practice of virtue."[5] The writer must, then, involve and exercise his audience in certain emotional responses that are calculated to further his didactic purpose.

Yet there is always the danger that the writer's emotional appeal will reap more harm than good. The same sensibility than can help to provide the means for the attainment of moral excellence can also, as we have observed, lead to corruption. The emotions are, after all, no infallible guide to human conduct but need to be conditioned and balanced by prudence and traditional morality—or by what Adam Smith calls the "general rules of conduct." Under the misnomer of sensibility, a person may delude himself into adopting equally inordinate modes of altruism or egotism. While Mackenzie's own faith in the moral efficacy of sensibility remains firm, we sense, nevertheless, an uneasy awareness of the risks involved. This ambivalence, as we have noted elsewhere, leads him to argue rather persuasively against romantic love and yet give these arguments to such unsympathetic as well as unreliable characters as Mrs. Boothby and Count Montauban.

In the *Mirror* and later in the *Lounger*, Mackenzie found a ready medium for giving expression to this growing concern, not only in reference to romantic love but relative to the whole problem of defining the province and limits of sensibility. In *Mirror*, No. 101, for example, entitled "Effects of sentiment and sensibility on happiness, from a guardian" (V, 1–17), he tells the story of Emilia through a letter from her distraught uncle:

> In books, whether moral or amusing, there are no passages more captivating both to the writer and the reader, than those delicate strokes of sentimental morality, which refer our actions to the determination of feeling. . . . I imagine, however, Sir, there is much danger in pushing these qualities too far; the rules of our conduct should be founded on a basis more solid, if they are to guide us through the various situations of life; but the young enthusiast of sentiment and feeling is apt to despise those lessons of vulgar virtue and prudence, which would confine the movements of a soul formed to regulate itself by finer impulses.

Emilia sacrifices her own happiness for the sake of her friendship for Harriet (who dies after an unhappy marriage to a fortune hunter) when she gives "to the dying charge of Harriet the romantic interpretation of becoming the wife of her widower, and the mother of her children." For Mackenzie, such self-abnegation went beyond good sense: "there are bounds beyond which virtuous feelings cease to be virtue . . . the decisions of sentiment are subject to the controul of prudence, and the ties of friendship subordinate to the obligations of duty."

The "sentimental novels" he condemns in "On Novel-writing" encourage such excesses by subverting the traditional values and priorities of moral conduct. In their "war of duties," preference is always given to the more unusual, the more sensational motive in lieu of that which seems common and mundane: "The duty to parents is contrasted with the ties of friendship and of love; the virtues of justice, of prudence, of economy, are put in competition with the exertions of generosity, of benevolence, and of compassion: and even of these virtues of sentiment there are still more refined divisions, in which the overstrained delicacy of the persons represented always leads them to act from the motive least obvious, and therefore generally the least reasonable."

Mirror, No. 101, and papers of a similar nature were intended as a corrective to such fictional representations.[6] Emilia sacrifices only herself at the altar of sensibility, but this makes her story all the more pathetic, and the religious parallel did not escape Mackenzie: "sentiment, like religion, had its superstition, and its martydom. Every hardship she suffered she accounted a trial, every censure she endured she considered as a testimony of her virtue." The Puritan's justification by faith in his own election has become justification by faith in his own goodness.

Yet, if the self-esteem of sensibility can lead one votary to categorical self-denial, it can help another to escape all moral obligations. Once again choosing his analogy from religion, Mackenzie warns in *Lounger*, No. 20:

> In the enthusiasm of sentiment there is much the same danger as in the enthusiasm of religion, of substituting certain impulses and feelings of what may be called a visionary kind, in the place of real practical duties, which in morals, as in theology, we might not improperly denominate good works. In morals, as in religion, there are not wanting instances of refined sentimentalists, who are contented with talking of virtues which they never practise, who pay in words what they owe in actions; or, perhaps, what is fully as dangerous, who open their minds to impressions which never have any effect upon their conduct, but are considered as something foreign to and distinct from it.[7]

Though Mackenzie blurs the distinction, he is describing two types of mock sensibility: one is the product of hypocrisy; the other stems from self-deception. The first is best exemplified by Diana Danby in *False Shame*, but hypocrisy also characterizes such rakes as Winbrooke in *The Man of Feeling* and Sindall in *The Man of the World*. Each feigns sensibility to deceive or to gain an advantage over his victim. From such deliberate duplicity, it is an easy step to the "sentimentalist" who has, in part at least, convinced himself of the disinterested spontaneity of his emotional responses and who voices them in those emotional reflections that Mackenzie's era revered under the denomination of *sentiments*.[8] The case is well illustrated by Mlle. Dorville as Savillon describes her in *Julia*: "There is a little world of sentiment made for women to move in, where they certainly excel our sex, and where our sex ought, perhaps, to be excelled by them. This is irresistibly engaging, where it is natural; but, of all affectations, that of sentiment is the most disgusting. It is, I believe, more common in France than any where else; and I am not sure if it does not proceed from our women possessing the reality less. The daughter of Mons. Dorville, when she would be great, is always sentimental" (III, 242).

A much more serious perversion of sensibility is described by William Craig, Mackenzie's intimate friend, in *Lounger*, No. 77: "A man may take pleasure in the passive feelings of sensibility, if that expression may be used, when he will avoid every thing which requires active exertion. Hence the mind may be open to the feelings of compassion and tenderness, may take delight in indulging them, and by that means acquire great acuteness of sensibility, when it may harden and shut itself against every object, where the giving way to the feelings which such object produces requires real activity and exertion."

Finally, there is the story of Miss Nettletop told by David Hume (the philosopher's nephew) in *Lounger*, No. 55. Passionate by nature, she has found in the cult of sensibility a convenient rationalization for her peevish disposition "under the more pleasing form of excessive delicacy." The origin of her delusion stems from the fashion current in her youth: "Owing I believe to certain novels then recently published, and in the very height of their popularity, the style of conversation was wholly sentimental; and the women universally vied one with another, in which they were imitated by some of the men, in making proof of the strength and the delicacy of their feeling." We are reminded of Lady Louisa Stuart's fear in reading *The Man of Feeling* lest she didn't "cry enough to gain the credit of proper sensibility." Miss Nettletop's affectation is, however, of a more serious nature because the pose soon becomes a reality for her: "The Gospels of Sentiment . . . were never out of her hands; she had their texts and phraseology at all times in her mouth; and thus by perpetual indulgence in one melting strain, having in time persuaded herself that she was in truth one of the tenderest and most refined of human beings, she gave herself up at last entirely to the direction of her feelings as instinctive guides, far surer and more infallible than observation or reflection."

At the end of Hume's letter, Mackenzie comments editorially: "Nothing is so provoking as this refined ill-humour, which takes the merit of sensibility from selfishness, and feels for every distress but those which it might cure." By now his standard of judgment is clear: true sensibility depends upon achieving a moral equilibrium between the extremes of self-interest and self-denial; it does not consist of passively indulging in emotions but of actively engaging in "good works" without losing a sense of prudence. Such is Mackenzie's portrait of Benevolus in *Lounger*, No. 96: "he gives largely; but as it is neither from the impulse of sickly sentiment, or shallow vanity, his largesses tend oftener to incite industry than to supply indigence."

Mackenzie's ideals, in short, are the traditional principles of moral conduct, which he saw threatened in the final decades of his century by the growing popularization and perversion of sensibility.[9] The vehemence of his attack on "sentimental" novelists stems from his fears that they were eroding these values and, what is worse, encouraging the cultivation of the emotions for their own sake. "This separation of conscience from feeling" leads him to insist on a narrow definition for sensibility and to denominate aberrations from it as "sickly" or "affected." From passages already quoted, we can see that Mackenzie frequently describes such abuses as *sentimental.* He refers to "sentimental novels" and "refined sentimentalists" in an obviously derogatory manner. Mlle. Dorville is characterized as "sentimental" for affecting sentiments, and the hypocritical Diana Danby is called a "sentimentalist." His ironic and often clearly pejorative use of a term that had come to be identified with the cult of sensibility is an attempt to dissociate the moral concept from the sham forms into which it had degenerated.

In this respect, it is noteworthy to observe that even Mrs. Boothby's "prudent argument," previously quoted, tends to associate *sentimental* with self-deception: "From being accustomed to admire a set of opinions, which they [young people] term sentimental, opposed to others, which they look upon as vulgar and unfeeling, they form to themselves an ideal system of those matters, which, from the nature of things, must always be disappointed" (II, 243). In *Lounger*, No. 20, some twelve years later, Mackenzie makes a similar point in delineating the psychological effects that "sentimental novelists" have upon readers: "That sickly sort of refinement creates imaginary evils and distresses, and imaginary blessings and enjoyments, which embitter the common disappointments, and depreciate the common attainments of life. This affects the temper doubly, both with respect to ourselves and others; with respect to ourselves, from what we think ought to be our lot; with regard to others, from what we think ought to be their sentiments."

If I have dwelled at length on Mackenzie's attitude toward sensibility, it has been in order to resolve its seeming contradictions rather than to imply its singularity. His concern with the moral degeneration of sensibility is, in fact, a central issue toward the end of the century that was voiced by others in the literature and periodicals of the period. Writing in the *Critical Review* in 1789, a reviewer contends:

> Yet, however highly we admire a well-directed sensibility; and think
> "That those who sow in tears shall reap in joy;"
> we are no less disgusted with the abuse of it. When indulged beyond the bounds of reason it degenerates into weakness; when affected, it is absurd; and when directed to improper objects, extremely dangerous. This word, like *sentiment*, has of late years been often strangely perverted, and applied to gild the violation of the most sacred duties. Excess of sensibility, or a sentimental affection, is often an apology for a young lady's elopement from a harsh father, or that of a wife from a stupid husband. *Delicate feelings* become the substitute for those of virtue; and we are too often taught by the prevalence of fashion and delusions of sophistry, to interest ourselves as much in the calamities of guilt, as in the affliction of innocence.[10]

Near the end of his essay, Mackenzie turns his attention to the question of whether or not characters of "mingled virtue and vice" ought to be introduced into the novel. Though he grants that a mixed character may prove more entertaining than a simple representation of good or evil, the mixed character, nevertheless, wields a pernicious influence because it "nourishes and supports a very common kind of self-deception, by which men are apt to balance their faults by the consideration of their good qualities." In his insistence on exemplary characterization and on the didactic role of the novelist, he again echoes Dr. Johnson's position.[11] What is far more significant, however, is that Mackenzie entirely ignores the novelist's obligation to realism just as he had shunned it in much of his own fiction. "The *real life*," Robert Chambers pointed out in 1840, "fashion had forbidden, and he [Mackenzie] had not the force to break through the rules of that tawdry deity. . . . As works of art, the novels and minor stories of Mackenzie are exquisite; but, nevertheless, they could never have attained so great a celebrity, if they had not appeared at a time when mere art was chiefly regarded by the public, and when, as yet, men esteemed nature as something not exactly fitted for drawing-room intercourse."[12]

II *An Examination of the Moral Effects of Tragedy*

Though entitled "On Novel-writing," *Lounger*, No. 20, actually examines, as we have seen, the moral effect the novel has upon its readers. Seven issues later in *Lounger*, Nos. 27–28,[13] Mackenzie turned his attention once more to the question of the moral efficacy of literature, this time in reference to tragedy. Even more so than before, his moralistic approach is essentially psychological since he is investigating the ways tragedy affects the mind of the reader or spectator. His conclusions form a severe attack on the didactic value of tragedy that comes as something of a surprise from the author of *The Prince of Tunis* and two other tragedies. Yet, as in *Lounger*, No. 20, Mackenzie is speaking in the customary role of moralist associated with periodical essayists rather than as a critic or as a playwright. The difference between the two essays stems from the traditional values the eighteenth century attributed to each of the genres: inasmuch as the novel was commonly condemned as a morally corrupting form of literature, Mackenzie's critique hardly constituted a new departure; on the other hand, to deny the moral efficacy of tragedy was to run counter to one of the basic tenets of neo-Classic criticism.

Though there was disagreement about the nature of tragedy's didactic role, as well as about the means utilized to effect such an end, its inherent moral value was generally agreed upon. Tragedy, John Dryden argues, "reform[s] manners by delightful representation of human life in great persons, by way of dialogue. If this be true, then not only pity and terror are to be moved as the only means to bring us to virtue, but generally love to virtue and hatred to vice; by showing the rewards of one, and punishments of the other; at least by rendering virtue always amiable, though it be shown unfortunate; and vice detestable, tho' it be shown triumphant."[14] For Joseph Addison, well-written tragedies "wear out of our Thoughts every thing that is mean and little. They cherish and cultivate that Humanity which is the Ornament of our Nature. They soften Insolence, sooth Affliction, and subdue the Mind to the Dispensations of Providence."[15]

Mackenzie's contemporaries voice similar ideas about the moral efficacy of tragedy. Lord Kames, for example, claims that "a pathetic composition, whether epic or dramatic, tends to a habit of virtue, by exciting us to do what is right, and restraining us from what is wrong. Its frequent pictures of human woe, produce, besides, two effects extremely salutary: they improve our sympathy, and fortify us to bear our own misfortunes. A moral composition obviously produces the same good effects, because by being moral it ceases not to be pathetic: it enjoys beside an excellence peculiar to itself; for it not only improves the heart as above mentioned, but instructs the head by the moral it contains."[16] Hugh Blair, in his *Lectures on Rhetoric and Belles Lettres* (1783), goes so far as to insist that "no reasonable person can deny tragedy to be a moral species of composition. Taking tragedies complexly, I am fully persuaded, that the impressions left by them upon the mind are, on the whole, favourable to virtue and good dispositions."[17]

Mackenzie's own discussion of tragedy, published two years later, is in some respects a rebuttal to Blair's argument, whose defense of tragedy rests in part on the claim that "no kind of writing has so much power, when happily executed, to raise the strongest emotions."[18] Since the passions are for Blair "the great springs of human action,"[19] such power enables tragedy to become a potent moral instrument. Mackenzie, on the other hand, attributes tragedy's corrupting influence to that very emotive capacity which Blair praises. Deeds that in real life are instinctively abhorred become attractive and even alluring within the rarefied atmosphere of tragedy: "Scenes presenting passions and vices, round which the poet throws the veil of magnanimity, which he decorates with the pomp of verse, with the splendor of eloquence, familiarise the mind to their appearance, and take from it that natural disgust which the crimes, presented in their native form, would certainly excite." Our repugnance for obvious vices is allayed when they become the attributes of the central protagonist with whom our sympathy is always to be found since "he must always be the hero on whom the principal stress of the action lies." For Blair, man's very nature precluded this danger:

> Such power hath virtue happily over the human mind by the wise and gracious constitution of our nature, that as admiration cannot be raised in epic poetry, so neither in tragic poetry can our passions be strongly moved, unless virtuous emotions be awakened within us. Every poet finds, that it is impossible to interest us in any character, without representing that character as worthy and honourable, though it may not be perfect; and that the great secret for raising indignation, is to paint the person who is to be the object of it, in the colours of vice and depravity.[20]

Mackenzie rejects such idealism because he always remains conscious of what I have elsewhere called "the dark side of sensibility"—that man's emotions could be the means to pervert his nature as well as to improve it. It is this realization that makes his evaluation of tragedy so severe a condemnation. Turning aside from the traditional defenses of tragedy that a century of neo-Classic criticism had developed, Mackenzie approached his subject empirically by focusing his attention upon the audience's reaction: how does tragedy affect the reader or spectator? As such, his essay becomes one of the most original discussions of tragedy in the latter part of the century.

Assuming the persona of a strict moralist, Mackenzie proceeds to condemn modern tragedy without suggesting a corrective because, as he clearly implies, the taste and expectation of a modern audience lead almost inevitably to a corrupt theater. Indeed, the very realities of dramatic representation require a certain heightening of normal emotional responses in order to affect the spectator. Yet such amplification, Mackenzie insists, results in protagonists who overreact to their own misfortunes, as does Castalio in Otway's *The Orphan* when he "is mad with anguish and with rage, because his wife's maid refuses him access to her apartment, according to the previous appointment they had made." Such inordinate displays of passions "have a tendency to weaken our mind to our own sufferings, without opening it to the sufferings of others. The real evils which the dignity of the scene hides from our view, are those which we ought to pity in our neighbours; the fantastic and imaginary distresses which it exhibits, are those we are apt to indulge in ourselves. Here then tragedy adds to the list of our calamities, without increasing the catalogue of our virtues."

Just as tragedy can lend dignity to excessive anguish, so it also tends to elevate indiscriminately a character's actions. "But this," Mackenzie points out, "removes virtue at a greater distance from us, and brings vice nearer; it exalts the first to a point beyond our imitation, and ennobles the latter to a degree above our abhorrence." Thus "Macbeth, a tyrant and a murderer," arouses our pity rather than our hate. Blair had claimed that modern tragedy, "by becoming more the theatre of passion," proved to be more edifying than Classical tragedy. Examples like Othello and Otway's Jaffier, he argued, show men the dangerous consequences of unbridled or misdirected emotions.[21] Mackenzie quotes Blair's argument, ascribing it to "a celebrated critic," and then proceeds to challenge his thesis by contending that it is an audience's total emotional response to a drama, the direction of their sympathy, that determines a play's moral value: "I am afraid, if we appeal to the feelings of the audience at the conclusion of any of those pieces, we shall not find the effect to be what is here supposed. Othello we rather pity for his jealousy, than hate as a murderer. With Jaffier and his associates we are undoubtedly leagued against the rulers of Venice;[22] and even the faith and tenderness of Belvidera hardly make us forgive her for betraying their secret" in Otway's *Venice Preserved* (1682).

While the critique of *Venice Preserved* is probably valid, Mackenzie's condemnation of *Macbeth* and *Othello* clearly reveals his narrow critical doctrine. For him, the function of tragedy is to arouse merely pity through scenes of human misery. The moral effect is achieved by directing the spectator's sympathy toward innocent and virtuous victims and his hatred toward the agents of their suffering. Taken from such a perspective, Shakespeare perverts his tragedies when he allows us to pity rather than hate a Macbeth and an Othello. Mackenzie, of course, fails to recognize that the moral effect in such drama, what Lord Kames calls *moral tragedy*, depends upon a combination of pity and terror: "our pity is engaged for the persons represented; and our terror is upon our own account."[23] Mackenzie insists on judging every tragedy by the standards of *pathetic tragedy*, a drama "that has nothing in view but to move the passions and to exhibit pictures of virtue and vice."[24]

The result of such a dramatic theory is, of course, all too evident in Mackenzie's own tragedies, written more than a decade earlier. Attention is nearly always focused upon the sufferer, the victim rather than the antagonist: King Rodriguez and Barbarossa are shadowy figures whose inner struggles are never explored and adequately dramatized because Mackenzie fails to recognize the moral value of such psychological conflict. He depicts in his dramas a simplistic view of good and evil, and he condemns modern tragedy for having blurred that distinction: whereas Classical tragedy clearly differentiated between virtue and vice, "the refinement of modern audiences calls for shades of character more delicate . . . the consequence is, that the bounds of right and wrong are often so uncertainly marked, as not to be easily distinguished." The young and inexperienced cannot be expected to make the proper distinction, particularly if the playwright has made vice alluring.

This concern—the psychological effect of depicting evil, even if only momentarily, in attractive or merely neutral colors—is at the root of Mackenzie's critique. The demands of dramatic representation require, of course, that a character's sentiments be consistent with his personality and situation. Yet "to give them this propriety," Mackenzie complains, "they must often be apologies for vice and for fraud, or contain ridicule against virtue and honesty." It matters little if such a character eventually meets his punishment, for, "if the sentiments at the time are shrewdly imagined, and forcibly expressed, they will have a powerful effect on the mind, and leave impressions which the retribution of poetical justice will hardly be able to efface." Once again Mackenzie fails to distinguish between *pathetic* and *moral* tragedies. His argument may have merit in reference to such outright villains as Edmund and Iago, but can the same be said for a tragic hero like Macbeth or Othello? Merely to punish the villain at the end of the play may fail to counteract the corrupting effect his dramatic presence has offered; however, when that retribution is the direct consequence of his own weaknesses, the moral lesson his fate suggests is likely to negate whatever attraction his vices have produced.

Mackenzie's position again confirms what we have already observed in his own tragedies: his whole concept of drama is rhetorical rather than discursive. Individual scenes are designed and arranged to produce a specific emotional effect rather than an instructive causal pattern. Hence he can argue against poetic justice on the ground that its absence will be more conducive to feelings of sympathy and hate: "I incline to be of the opinion of one of my predecessors, that we are frequently more roused to a love of virtue, and hatred of vice, when virtue is unfortunate, and vice successful, than when each receives the recompence it merits." Mackenzie is probably referring to William Craig who, in *Mirror,* No. 77, contends that every human desire "gathers new strength by opposition, and rises upon resistance." It follows from this principle that where virtue remains unrewarded, it "attaches us so much the more warmly to its interests; and that, where vice is successful, instead of creating a feeling in its favour, this only increases our indignation against it."

Tragedy is thus seen as an instrument by which to manipulate the emotions of the spectator, and we are not far from the melodrama of the next century where the heroine is to be wept over while we hiss at the villain. Such drama tends to flatter an audience's ego; since characters are represented in purely white and black terms, a spectator is unlikely to feel any identity with evil. Hence pity is reserved for the good, while fear for ourselves, lest we fall into similar evil, is converted to simple hate for the evildoer.

Where the lines between vice and virtue are so distinctly drawn, all dramatic conflict is by necessity externalized. For Mackenzie, however, this externalization was all to the good because it eliminated a troublesome problem he had encountered in his own plays. To justify the weakness of a Clarissa or Calista, villains like Lovelace or Lothario had to be made attractive and given some pleasing attributes: "The story would not be probable else;—granted; but in proportion to the art of the poet in rendering it probable, he heightens the immoral effect of which I complain." As a playwright, Mackenzie had sought to solve this problem by conceiving his antagonists as villains of passion who are swayed and manipulated by much more evil villains of principle. Yet, as a moralist concerned with the effect of tragedy upon youth, he was willing to sacrifice probability for the sake of insulating the spectator.

Curiously enough, though, Mackenzie could in the same essay condemn tragedy for both its idealization of life and its lack of utility. The virtues of tragic characters "are not so much the useful, the productive virtues (if I may be allowed the expression) of real life, as the shining and showy qualities, which attract the applause, or flatter the vanity, of the unthinking." Neither are tragic scenes of human suffering and misery either applicable to real life or edifying, though Mackenzie's contemporaries defended tragedy upon such grounds. Lord Kames argued that "its frequent pictures of human woe ... improve our sympathy"; Blair claimed that tragedy tended "to improve our virtuous sensibility," in part through "compassion for the distressed";[25] but Mackenzie denied such utility on the ground that poets aggrandize their heroes' afflictions to the point where they are no longer relevant to common life.

If anything, such dramatizations of human woe produce a negative effect upon the spectator: "He who is deeply conversant in the tragic phrase, in the swelling language of compassion, of generosity, and of love, finding no parallel in his common intercourse with mankind, will not so readily open his heart to the calls on his feeling, which the vulgar distresses of his fellow-creatures, or the ordinary relations of life, may occasion." Here again the poet's desire to please his audience makes the situation almost inevitable: since "real calamity offends with its coarseness," as the unpopularity of George Lillo's *Fatal Curiosity* and Edward Moore's *The Gamester* attests, the stage "exhibits in its stead the fantastic griefs of a delicate and high-wrought sensibility."

At the end of the essay, Mackenzie anticipates the likely reaction of his reader: "I shall be asked, if I mean to prescribe every novel and every tragedy, or of what kind of each I am disposed to allow the perusal, and to what class of readers their perusal may be trusted." He approaches this problem from the same psycho-moralistic perspective from which the rest of his essay has been developed. Works of fiction and drama may be beneficial and prove a corrective for those of an insensitive and hence egotistical disposition: "The region of exalted virtue, of dignified sentiment, into which they transport us, may have a considerable effect in changing the cold and unfeeling temperament of worldly minds; the indifferent and the selfish may be warmed and expanded by the fiction of distress, and the eloquence of feeling."

Literature, it may be noted, is here recommended not for its direct applicability to life but rather as a therapeutic device that serves to increase the natural sensibility of the reader. As such, it is in marked contrast to Mackenzie's own fiction, which, he had implied, was designed for the emotionally responsive reader who alone could appreciate men of Harley's temperament. An additional and much more significant difference between the idealistic writer and the empirical moralist is to be seen in the assumption that men of "cold and unfeeling temperament" have the capacity for change. In Mackenzie's own tragedies, such a psychological principle is inoperative; his villains of principle, with the possible exception of Sindall, are stark and consistent figures of evil without any capability of regeneration.

Equally paradoxical is the fact that Mackenzie is least willing to trust the kind of reader for whom his own work of fiction and drama had had their greatest appeal: "There is a certain sort of mind common in youth, and that too of the most amiable kind, tender, warm, and visionary, to which the walks of fancy and enthusiasm, of romantic love, of exaggerated sorrow, of trembling sensibility, are very unsafe." Yet his conclusion is consistent with the tenor of his argument: if tragedy influences the spectator or reader by appealing to his passions, the person most easily affected and hence most likely to be corrupted would be the one having the most intense emotional susceptibility. "In such bosoms," Mackenzie advises, "feeling or susceptibility must be often repressed or directed; to encourage it by premature or unnatural means, is certainly hurtful." We are reminded of Harriet Annesly, who "would often weep all night from some tale . . . of fictitious disaster." Mackenzie, in fact, suggests such an association by closing his essay with a paraphrase from the *The Man of the World*: "They [sensitive readers] resemble some luxuriant soils, which may be enriched beyond a wholesome fertility, till weeds are their only produce; weeds, the more to be regretted, as, in the language of a novelist himself, 'they grow in the soil from which virtue should have sprung.'"[26]

III *Observations on Comedy*

Though the *Lounger* essays on comedy comprise two papers, Mackenzie composed only No. 50, January 4, 1786 (VI, 3–15). *Lounger*, No. 49, written by William Craig, deals with the history and development of ancient and modern comedy. Mackenzie's approach to comedy closely resembles the method he had already developed in his examination of fiction and tragedy. He again assumes the rigid role of moralist whose primary concern is to judge the didactic effectiveness of comedy—what is its psychological effect upon an audience? Mackenzie begins with a traditional definition: "Comedy wishes to purge vices and follies, by ridicule." But, he is quick to add, ridicule may become a two-edged sword by attacking morality rather than defending it: "At every age, reason and duty are grave and serious things, in which ridicule finds a contrast that renders her attack more easy, and her sallies more poignant." Needless to say, Mackenzie opposes the doctrine of ridicule as a test of truth,[27] a question that was debated throughout the century;[28] but his attitude toward the third earl of Shaftesbury, the originator of the doctrine,[29] is only mildly critical: "I never thought Shaftesbury so dangerou[s a] Writer as some People hold him; there is a Freedom of Enquiry no doubt in his Works; & his setting out w^{t} the Defence of Ridicule as a proper Weapon of Argument was naturally alarming to serious Men; but I am never much afraid of an Author friendly to the finer Virtues."[30]

Just as Mackenzie had attacked modern tragedy for blurring "the bounds of right and wrong," he found a similar lack of distinction in the subjects of present-day comedy: "They paint those nicer shades of ridicule, which are of an equivocal sort, between virtue and vice, and often give the spectator leave to laugh, according to his own humour, either at the first or the latter." There is, in fact, enough disparity between comic representations and real life to allow the spectator to either evade or pervert the object of ridicule: "The images which comedy presents, and the ridicule which it excites, being almost always exaggerated, their resemblance to real life is only acknowledged by those whose weaknesses they flatter—whose passions they excuse." Though Molière condemns Harpagon in *The Miser,* the play will not turn any spectator away from avarice, for "misers and usurers neither read nor see comedies." Instead, it encourages those of a prodigal temperament "to call prudence and economy, covetousness and avarice, to be dissipated and extravagant out of pure virtue." Though most of Mackenzie's examples are derived from Molière, he is not necessarily condemning his plays. Elsewhere, in fact, he ranks Molière above all other comic playwrights because he "gives the reader as well as the spectator the most perfect delight from the justness of his characters and the electric strokes of the dialogue by which the portraits are distinguished."[31] Mackenzie is merely judging the moral efficacy of the genre, as he had previously judged the novel and tragedy. Comedy, he is saying, by the very nature of its conventions proves to be an ineffective didactic device.

A traditional servant-rogue, such as Scapin in Molière's *Les Fourberies de Scapin,* corrupts the young in the audience more effectively than a real servant because they see a character on the stage who is not only more attractive and ingenious but who is encouraged in his dupery by members of the upper class who benefit from his mischief. Such a corrupting effect depends, however, on theatrical representation since "ridicule operat[es] more powerfully in company, and in a crowd." Tragedy, on the other hand, does not require dramatization to be effective; "on the contrary, it is perhaps in the reading that it fastens most strongly on young and susceptible minds. The softer feelings . . . are more accessible in solitude and silence than in society." But, if for the reader comedy represents less danger than tragedy, for the spectator comedy proves more harmful. Comedy offers more verisimilitude in its characterizations because, while "no hero of a player [is]) equal to the hero of a tragedy . . . the handsome figure, the showy garb, the assured countenance, the unembarrassed address, the easy negligence, of many a comedian, is fully equal to the character he is to represent." Such similitude, Mackenzie wittily suggests, stems from the fact that "the fine gentleman of real life is a sort of comic actor." This realism of portrayal makes the dialogue effective and the hero so attractive as to gloss over his shortcomings.

Such realism is all the more to be feared because of the means by which dramatic conflict is resolved in comedy. Marriage always closes the action, but it is generally decided upon impulsively without forethought or judgment. For Mackenzie the moralist, the convention of "love at first sight" is obviously pernicious as is the complementary tendency of comedy to ridicule "an union . . . of tried attachment, of sober preference, sanctified by virtue, and by prudence." Equally disturbing and detrimental is the fact that comedy's traditional conflict of generations always favors youth: "age, wisdom, experience, every thing which a well-educated young person should respect and venerate, is made a jest of; pertness, impudence, falsehood, and dishonesty, triumph and laugh; the audience triumphs and laughs along with them; and it is not till within a few sentences of the conclusion, that the voice of morality is uttered, not heard." At that point, the audience is ready to leave; and, if anyone listens at all, he does so only to note "how dull and common-place" the words are.

Near the end of the essay Mackenzie turns his attention to "some of our latest comedies." These, he contends, are far more immoral than Restoration comedies ever were: "those sometimes violated decency, but these attack principle; those might put modesty to the blush, or contaminate the purity of innocence; but these shake the very foundations of morality, and would harden the mind against the sense of virtue. . . . Figaro, though a less witty, is as immoral a play as the School for Scandal." He blames the emergence of such plays "upon the fashionable ridicule against what was called Sentimental Comedy, which it had become customary to decry, as subverting the very intention of that department of the stage, and usurping a name, from which the gravity of its precepts, and the seriousness of its incidents, should have excluded it." Mackenzie is defending a genre or specifically the introduction of didactic situations and sententious dialogue into comedy. His stand is hardly surprising when we view his three genre essays together. Consistent in his moralistic position, he judges each genre, in turn, for its didactic efficacy. Yet such an approach forms a marked contrast to his two papers on Shakespeare.

IV *Criticism on the Character of Hamlet*

The first of Mackenzie's essays on Shakespeare and the only one to have received critical attention[32] is his examination of Hamlet's character that appeared in *Mirror,* Nos. 99–100, on April 18 and 22, 1780 (IV, 371–95). Mackenzie begins his observations by noting Hamlet's seemingly inconsistent character: "With the strongest purposes of revenge, he is irresolute and inactive; amidst the gloom of the deepest melancholy, he is gay and jocular; and while he is described as a passionate lover, he seems indifferent about the object of his affections." Mackenzie's task will be "to enquire, whether any leading idea can be found, upon which these apparent contradictions may be reconciled." Not surprisingly, he finds the key to Hamlet's personality to be "an extreme sensibility of mind, apt to be strongly impressed by its situation, and overpowered by the feelings which that situation excites." Such a nature is most apt to become disillusioned by the particular events Hamlet experiences—a mother's disloyalty and an uncle's treachery. Indeed, Mackenzie suggests that the action of the play is deliberately designed to display Hamlet's highly wrought sensibility: "Finding such a character in real life, of a person endowed with feelings so delicate as to border on weakness, with sensibility too exquisite to allow of determined action, he [Shakespeare] has placed it where it could be best exhibited, in scenes of wonder, of terror, and of indignation, where its varying emotions might be most strongly marked amidst the workings of imagination and the war of the passions."

It is a truism of Shakespearean criticism that his commentators often reveal as much about themselves and their times as they do about the plays before them, and Mackenzie is no exception. If we recall his purpose in composing his first novel—he wanted to introduce "a man of sensibility into different scenes where his feelings might be seen in their effects"—we can see how much his own literary theory colored his interpretation of *Hamlet.* Just as his own tragedies abound in scenes designed to evoke the passions of his protagonists, so is Shakespeare assumed to follow a similar purpose. The ghost is thus introduced because Hamlet's reaction to his speech is "aptly suited to display the wavering purpose, and varied emotions, of a mind endowed with a delicacy of feeling that often shakes its fortitude, with sensibility that overpowers its strength."

But why, Mackenzie asks, has the poet endowed Hamlet with such debilitating qualities when his prototype, the "Amleth of Saxo-Grammaticus," acts with resolution and shrewdness? Shakespeare, he suggests, wanted his audience to identify with his hero by arousing their sympathy; hence he "throws around him, from the beginning, the majesty of melancholy, along with that sort of weakness and irresolution which frequently attends it." A determined Hamlet, impeded only by external circumstances, would have created concern; "but it would have been anxiety for the event, not for the person." Like Orestes, he would have been a mere "instrument of . . . justice." "As it is, we feel not only the virtues, but the weaknesses of Hamlet, as our own."

Within such an interpretation, Hamlet's procrastination becomes largely a product of his melancholy rather than the result of his shrewdness. Fear lest the devil has assumed his father's shape is to be regarded as the rationalization of a vacillating mind; for "this doubt of the grounds on which our purpose is founded, is as often the effect, as the cause, of irresolution, which first hesitates, and then seeks out an excuse for its hesitation."

But if we accept such self-deception and melancholy as characterizing Hamlet's state of mind, the question naturally arises of how far his seeming madness is actually pretense. Up to 1770, critics had generally accepted his derangement as feigned and self-controlled, though they often questioned the logic of his strategy. In the last decades of the century, however, Hamlet was increasingly viewed as at times possessing or approaching the very madness he tries to assume.[33]

Mackenzie rejected such an interpretation, claiming that Hamlet's "distraction . . . is clearly affected through the whole play; always subject to the controul of his reason, and subservient to the accomplishment of his designs." His assumption is based on a comparison of *Hamlet* and *King Lear*: the difference between Lear's real madness and Edgar's feigned distraction is that the former harps obsessively on the main sources of his grief—the ingratitude of his daughters and the abdication of his power—while Edgar takes care never to give expression to his "ruling thoughts." Similarly, Ophelia, after growing mad, becomes preoccupied with the death of her father, while Hamlet tries to suppress his "reigning impressions"—his love for Ophelia and the treachery of his uncle. However, lacking Edgar's self-control and stability, his "counterfeited madness . . . could not be so uniformly kept up, as not to allow the reigning impressions of his mind to shew themselves in the midst of his affected extravagance." Though ingenious, Mackenzie provides little internal evidence to support his argument. He ignores, moreover, the problem of defining insanity: at what point does emotional instability become a definite aberration and a threat to one's sanity?

Curiously enough, after claiming that Hamlet lacks the force of will to hide entirely his deepest feelings, Mackenzie takes the very opposite position to prove that the prince's abusive treatment of Ophelia does not throw doubt on his love for her. In fact, his harshness supposedly demonstrates just the contrary: "Feeling its [his affection for her] real force, and designing to play the madman on that ground, he would naturally go as far from the reality as possible." Mackenzie may have been trying to answer Dr. Johnson's observation that Hamlet's treatment of Ophelia "seems to be useless and wanton cruelty," but that point rests on Johnson's prior contention that there is no "adequate cause" for his counterfeit madness,[34] a question that Mackenzie chose to ignore.

Nor is his defense of Hamlet entirely original. Six years before, William Richardson had pointed out that Hamlet, in order to seem deranged, "would act in direct opposition to his former conduct, and inconsistently with the genuine sentiments and affections of his soul. . . . To Ophelia he would shew dislike and indifference; because a change of this nature would be, of all others, the most remarkable, and because his affection for her was passionate and sincere."[35] Mackenzie, however, refines upon Richardson's argument with a subtle insight into human nature: "Had he not loved her at all, or slightly loved her, he might have kept up some appearance of passion amidst his feigned insanity; but really loving her, he would have been hurt by such a resemblance in the counterfeit. We can bear a downright caricature of our friend much easier than an unfavourable likeness."[36]

A last contradiction to be resolved is how to account for Hamlet's occasional "gaiety and playfulness" amidst his general state of melancholy. To Mackenzie, no inconsistency exists if we understand the real nature of his state of mind: "That sort of melancholy which is the most genuine, as well as the most amiable of any, neither arising from natural sourness of temper, nor prompted by accidental chagrin, but the effect of delicate sensibility, impressed with a sense of sorrow, or a feeling of its own weakness, will, I believe, often be found indulging itself in a sportfulness of external behaviour, amidst the pressure of a sad, or even the anguish of a broken heart." From such a "sense of sorrow" stems likewise the detachment of Hamlet's wit and his reflections upon meeting the gravediggers and the army of Fortinbras.

In reading this part of his essay, we sense a note of conviction that sets it apart from his two earlier arguments. Mackenzie seems to speak here from an intimate knowledge of human nature rather than merely on the basis of deductive speculations. It is true that in most accounts of Mackenzie, he is described as an extrovert who bears little resemblance to his most famous character—Harley. "No man," wrote Sir Walter Scott in his journal, "is less known from his writings. We would suppose a retired, modest, somewhat affected man with a white handkerchief and a sigh ready for every sentiment. No such thing. H.M. is alert as a contracting tailor's needle in every sort of business, a politician and a sportsman, shoots and fishes in a sort even to this day [December 6, 1825], and is the life of the company with anecdotes and fun." But then Scott adds: "Sometimes his daughter tells me he is low in spirits at home but really I never see anything of it in Society."[37] Some of his own letters confirm this private side of his personality, as when he complains to his cousin about "undescribable Uneasinesses which I cannot overcome."[38]

Mackenzie, I suggest, saw certain affinities between Hamlet's state of mind and his own disposition, and this recognition gives his analysis its perspicacious, its almost clinical tone: "The melancholy man feels in himself (if I may be allowed the expression) a sort of double person; one which, covered with the darkness of its imagination, looks not forth into the world, nor takes any concern in vulgar objects or frivolous pursuits; another, which he lends, as it were, to ordinary men, which can accommodate itself to their tempers and manners, and indulge, without feeling any degradation from the indulgence, a smile with the cheerful, and a laugh with the giddy."

Mackenzie leaves us with the impression that Hamlet's melancholy, "along with that sort of weakness and irresolution which frequently attends it," results from a trauma that a man of his extreme sensibility would feel most keenly. In other words, the shock of having to recognize the true nature of his mother and uncle overpowers his spirit and debilitates his will. There are times, however, when Mackenzie, as we have seen, suggests that Hamlet's excessive delicacy has in itself enervated his character.

He speaks of "a person endowed with feelings so delicate as to border on weakness, with sensibility too exquisite to allow of determined action"; and, at the end of *Mirror*, No. 99, he again refers to "a mind endowed with a delicacy of feeling that often shakes its fortitude, with sensibility that overpowers its strength." The question arises then whether Hamlet's irresolution stems directly from his sensibility or is only the reaction of a mind of his disposition to a specific and overwhelming experience. On the one hand, excessive sensibility is in itself a psychological weakness while, on the other hand, it can under specific circumstances induce such mental debility. Mackenzie, though he puts more stress on the second view, is hardly consistent on this point; and his ambiguity reflects once again his own ambivalence toward sensibility.

The first of these interpretations is commonly associated with Goethe's famous description of Hamlet: "A lovely, pure, noble and most moral nature, without the strength of nerve which forms a hero, sinks beneath a burden which it cannot bear and must not cast away."[39] Although parts of the *Mirror* essay may have anticipated Goethe's concept, it is nevertheless Mackenzie's second view of Hamlet that is the more significant of the two. A. C. Bradley, who refers to Mackenzie as "the first of our critics to feel the 'indescribable charm' of Hamlet, and to divine something of Shakespeare's intention,"[40] shows Mackenzie's influence in his own interpretation. Bradley speaks of Hamlet's "moral sensibility" (earlier he had called it "exquisite sensibility") and the risk that "any great shock that life might inflict on it would be felt with extreme intensity": "suppose that under this shock, any possible action being denied to him, he began to sink into melancholy; then, no doubt, his imagination and generalising habit of mind might extend the effects of this shock through his whole being and mental world. And if, the state of melancholy being thus deepened and fixed, a sudden demand for difficult and decisive action in a matter connected with the melancholy arose, this state might well have for one of its symptoms an endless and futile mental dissection of the required deed."[41]

V *Critical Remarks on the Character of Falstaff*

Six years after his essay on Hamlet, Mackenzie once more ventured into Shakespearean criticism in his analysis of Falstaff in *Lounger*, Nos. 68–69, May 20 and 27, 1786 (VI, 148–70). Falstaff's singular nature, Mackenzie argues, stems from the way Shakespeare has combined "infinite wit and humour" and acute knowledge of human nature with "grossness of mind." Such a "strange compound" is perfectly suited to fulfill his purpose of alluring Hal: "With talents less conspicuous, Falstaff could not have attracted Henry; with profligacy less gross and less contemptible, he would have attached him too much. Falstaff's was just 'that unyoked humour of idleness,' which the Prince could 'a while uphold,' and then cast off for ever." Falstaff arouses both admiration and disgust in Hal, and the audience shares his ambivalent response to Falstaff.[42]

Despite such introductory remarks about Falstaff's function in *Henry IV,* Mackenzie views him as he had viewed Hamlet—a self-contained character with a life of his own apart from the scenes in which he appears. Mackenzie was thereby following, as we have stated, a pattern already set by Richardson, Whately, and Morgann. Though disagreeing with Morgann's contention that Falstaff possessed valor, Mackenzie shares his interest in "the *Impression* which the *whole* character of *Falstaff* is calculated to make on the minds of an unprejudiced audience." For Morgann, such an "impression" stems from "certain feelings or sensations of mind which do not seem to have passed thro' the Understanding."[43] For Mackenzie, the impression is a product of the reader's "congenial imagination" without which he can no more attain much pleasure from poetry than the poet can produce great literature: "The mind of him who reads, should be able to imagine what the productive fancy of the poet creates and presents to his view; to look on the world of fancy set before him with a native's eye, and to hear its language with a native's ear; to acknowledge its manners, to feel its passions, and to trace, with somewhat of an instinctive glance, those characters with which the poet has peopled it."

With such a "critical imagination," as he calls it, Mackenzie approaches Shakespeare's character and attempts to define his basic nature. Essentially, Falstaff is a "man of pleasure" whose ruling principle is "Epicurean grossness." Underlying his wit, Mackenzie finds a good-humored, even-tempered spirit: "The language of contempt, of rebuke, or of conviction, neither puts him out of liking with himself, or with others." He is, in fact, nearly indifferent to the judgment of other men: "The dread of disgrace, the sense of honour, and the love of fame, he neither feels, nor pretends to feel . . . he is contented to repose on that earthy corner of sensual indulgence in which his fate has placed him, and enjoys the pleasure of the moment, without once regarding those finer objects of delight, which the children of fancy and of feeling so warmly pursue."

No doubt such an interpretation has its flaws. The character of Falstaff is too enigmatic and the situations in which it unfolds in three plays are too diverse to make such a theory wholly unexceptionable.[44] Mackenzie has, nevertheless, hit upon a basic element in Falstaff's character, particularly as it is revealed in *Henry IV, Part I.* He anticipates, in fact, the amoral Falstaff that Benedetto Croce described more than a century later:

> Falstaff could call himself a "formal" hero in his own way: magnificent in ignoring morality and honour, logical, coherent, acute, and dexterous. He is a being in whom the sense of honour has never appeared, or has been obliterated, but the intellect has developed and become what alone it could become, namely, *esprit*, or sharpness of wit. He is without malice, because malice is the antithesis of moral conscientiousness, and he lacks both thesis and antithesis. There is in him, on the contrary, a sort of innocence, the result of the complete liberty of his relation toward all restraint and towards ethical law.[45]

Examining Falstaff within another context but arriving at similar conclusions, Franz Alexander writes in *Psychoanalytic Quarterly*: "He represents the deep infantile layers of the personality, the simple innocent wish to live and enjoy life. He has no taste for abstract values like honor or duty and no ambition. . . . Falstaff is the personification of the wholly self-centered pleasure-seeking principle. Although he represents the opposite of destruction, the principle of life, libido, it is the most primitive manifestation of libido, the primary self-centered, narcissistic libido of the child which he stands for."[46]

Mackenzie could not, of course, have read Freud; but he was, as we have seen, thoroughly familiar with Adam Smith's *Theory of Moral Sentiments*, which in some respects foreshadows modern psychological theory, particularly that of Freud.[47] For Smith, as we recall, the scrutiny and judgment of oneself depends upon an awareness that one's conduct is the object of other men's approval or censure. Society thus provides man with a "mirror" without which "he could no more think of his own character, of the propriety or demerit of his own sentiments and conduct, of the beauty or deformity of his own mind, than of the beauty or deformity of his own face."[48] The basic assumption underlying Smith's moral system is that man possesses an inherent regard for the judgment of his fellow beings.

This sensitivity to the estimate of other men, this need to seek their approval and avoid their censure, Falstaff lacks almost entirely, just as he is wanting in that power of the imagination which enables us to examine our own conduct "as we imagine an impartial spectator would examine it."[49] But this very deficiency is the source of Falstaff's characteristic prudence: he can counterfeit death with cool presence of mind because his cowardice is "not so much a weakness, as a principle." It "is only proportionate to the danger; and so would every wise man's be," Mackenzie adds, "did not other feelings make him valiant."[50] What induces men to act in a praiseworthy and disinterested manner, according to Smith, is the pleasure they receive from seeing themselves in the eyes of an impartial spectator as "the natural objects of approbation, though no approbation should ever actually be bestowed upon [them]."

The imagination likewise enables men to foretaste that glory which they are destined never to enjoy: "Men have often voluntarily thrown away life to acquire after death a renown which they could no longer enjoy. Their imagination, in the mean time, anticipated that fame which was thereafter to be bestowed upon them. Those applauses which they were never to hear rung in their ears; the thoughts of that admiration, whose effects they were never to feel, played about their hearts, banished from their breasts the strongest of all natural fears, and transported them to perform actions which seem almost beyond the reach of human nature."[51]

Human idealism thus rests to a large extent on the power of the imagination to transcend man's basic nature. Without such a capacity, the pursuit of honor, as Falstaff's "catechism" indicates, turns out to be mere human folly. But the imagination plays its role not only in acts of heroism; it likewise enables us to escape the mundane "pleasure of the moment" by directing our goals toward an unrealized future: "The greatest refinement of morals, as well as of mind, is produced by the culture and exercise of the imagination, which derives, or is taught to derive, its objects of pursuit, and its motives of action, not from the senses merely, but from future considerations, which fancy anticipates and realizes. Of this either as the prompter, or the restraint of conduct, Falstaff is utterly devoid; yet his imagination is wonderfully quick and creative in the pictures of humour, and the associations of wit."

What is most significant in Mackenzie's statement is that he attributes two distinct roles to the imagination—moral and hedonic. In the second case, the imagination creates wit by discovering novel resemblances between ideas. However, as Addison points out, "every Resemblance of Ideas is not that which we call Wit, unless it be such an one that gives *Delight* and *Surprise* to the Reader."[52] In serving the cause of wit, the imagination is then primarily a source of pleasure. To attribute such a function to Falstaff's imagination is, of course, consistent with Mackenzie's interpretation. Falstaff pleases his listeners with his wit, though he uses it to exploit them, shaping "his discourse according to the disposition of his hearers."

At the same time, Falstaff is destitute of that higher form of the imagination without which, Mackenzie argues, man becomes little more than a brute. As he states in *Lounger*, No. 100, entitled "Defence of literary studies and amusements in men of business," "the waste of time is undoubtedly a very calculable loss; but the waste or the depravation of mind is a loss of a much higher denomination. The votary of study, or the enthusiast of fancy, may incur the first; but the latter will be suffered chiefly by him whom ignorance, or want of imagination, has left to the grossness of mere sensual enjoyments" (VII, 24). Harley's highly developed imagination gives him, we recall, his characteristic compassion and benevolence because it enables him to change "places in fancy with the sufferer." This ability to enter into another's feelings by imaginatively putting oneself in his place, this *Mitfühlung* by which self-interest is temporarily subordinated to concern for others, Falstaff lacks entirely.

"None of his passions," Mackenzie tells us, "rise beyond this controul of reason, of self-interest, or of indulgence." There is, in fact, little of spontaneity in his character—all his actions are coldly deliberate and selfish: "He has neither the vanity of a wit, nor the singularity of a humourist, but indulges both talents, like any other natural propensity, without exertion of mind, or warmth of enjoyment." His role must, therefore, be played with "comic gravity" rather than with spontaneous mirth, for "he who laughs, is a man of feeling in merriment. Falstaff was of a very different constitution. He turned wit, as he says he did 'disease, into commodity.'" The same may be said of his love, as it is revealed in *The Merry Wives of Windsor*: it "is only factor for his interest, and he wishes to make his mistress 'his Exchequer, his East and West Indies, to both of which he will trade.'"

Yet, if Falstaff lacks these natural impulses that characterize "the children of fancy and of feeling," he possesses, Mackenzie begrudgingly concedes, extraordinary abilities. Remaining detached—immune to emotional involvement—makes Falstaff so coldly analytical that he seems to share Shakespeare's own "sagacity and penetration into the characters and motives of mankind." He likewise possesses an uncommonly agile wit and humor, though he uses these talents to demean human values and ideals, "subjecting wisdom, honour, and other the most grave and dignified principles, to the controul of grossness, buffoonery, and folly." We constantly sense here Mackenzie's ambivalent response to Shakespeare's character: the conservative moralist alarmed by the object of Falstaff's ridicule, the intuitive critic awed by the pure artistry of the characterization. "We are astonished at that art by which Shakespeare leads the powers of genius, imagination, and wisdom, in captivity to this son of the earth; it is as if, transported into the enchanted island in the Tempest, we saw the rebellion of Caliban successful, and the airy spirits of Prospero ministering to the brutality of his slave."

What is perhaps most remarkable in this interpretation is the way Mackenzie, near the close of the essay, builds upon his original concept to expand his subject and scope. Thomas Whately had compared Richard III with Macbeth because "none seem to agree so much in situation, and to differ so much in disposition."[53] Mackenzie, in turn, begins by showing how much similitude exists between Richard III and Falstaff and then proceeds to contrast both characters with Macbeth, thereby exploring the nature of that potential evil which lies dormant in Shakespeare's comic figure: "Both [Richard and Falstaff] despise those refined feelings, those motives of delicacy, those restraints of virtue, which might obstruct the course they have marked out for themselves. The hypocrisy of both costs them nothing, and they never feel that detection of it to themselves, which rankles in the consciences of less determined hypocrites. Both use the weaknesses of others, as skilfull players at a game do the ignorance of their opponents; they enjoy the advantage, not only without self-reproach, but with the pride of superiority."

In picturing Richard III as an insensitive, remorseless villain, Mackenzie is following the traditional eighteenth-century interpretation. Whately, for example, describes Richard as "totally destitute of every softer feeling"[54] and claims that, when he murders Clarence, "he feels no remorse for the deed, nor fear of discovery."[55] Mackenzie's originality lies in comparing Richard with Falstaff,[56] in seeing such striking affinities between seemingly dissimilar characters. Only their general temperaments distinguish them: "Richard indeed aspires to the crown of England, because Richard is wicked and ambitious: Falstaff is contented with a thousand pounds of Justice Shallow's, because he is only luxurious and dissipated." Yet this difference makes Richard what Mackenzie calls the "villain of principle," whereas Falstaff is "the knave and the sensualist" because, though equally amoral, he is too indolent to be "positively much a villain."

When Mackenzie proceeds to compare Richard with Macbeth, he again shows the influence of earlier critics; but he synthesizes their concepts to integrate them into his interpretation. What distinguishes Macbeth from both Richard and Falstaff is his emotional susceptibility. Macbeth is for Mackenzie, therefore, a villain of passion rather than a villain of principle. Whately suggests a similar distinction when, in contrast to Richard, he pictures Macbeth as "not destitute of the feelings of humanity" and ascribes his reluctance to murder Duncan to "reflexions which arise from sensibility."[57] Likewise, "the natural sensibility of his disposition" makes Macbeth refuse to fight Macduff; "he declines . . . not from fear, but from a consciousness of the wrongs he had done to him."[58]

A different and far more sophisticated interpretation is developed by William Richardson, who himself may have been influenced by Adam Smith. Macbeth's very sensibility, he argues, tends to make him more brutal and malevolent. Being able to conceive the indignation his crimes have inspired and fearing "the punishment he would himself have inflicted," he develops a much more violent hatred for mankind than would an insensitive person who can have no "lively conceptions, from his own feelings, of the resentment he has excited."[59] Mackenzie's interpretation is simpler though probably influenced by Richardson: Macbeth is "shown agitated by various and wavering emotions. He is sometimes more sanguinary than Richard, because he is not insensible of the weakness, or the passion of revenge; whereas the cruelty of Richard is only proportionate to the object of his ambition, as the cowardice of Falstaff is proportionate to the object of his fear: but the bloody and revengful Macbeth is yet susceptible of compassion, and subject to remorse."

It is, of course, not surprising that such a dichotomy of evil appeals to Mackenzie. In his own plays, we have seen a consistent pattern of villains of passion set off by villains of principle long before he coined the terms. It provided him with a flexible rhetorical tool through which to control his audience's reactions: "Macbeth produces horror, fear, and sometimes pity; Richard detestation and abhorrence only." Yet Mackenzie's essay is of wide significance quite apart from such considerations. By attributing a moral function to the imagination, he anticipated in some respects a basic assumption of Romantic criticism.[60] That is not to suggest that his concept was necessarily original, particularly in the Scotland of the last decades of the eighteenth century. Dugald Stewart, for example, argues that "the apparent coldness and selfishness of mankind may be traced, in a great measure, to a want of attention and a want of imagination."[61] Mackenzie's contribution lies rather in the use he made of Adam Smith's psychology of sympathy to develop a fresh and original approach to the enigma of Falstaff.

CHAPTER 8

Conclusion

HISTORIANS of the novel have long been accustomed to classify Henry Mackenzie as a disciple of Sterne and then proceed to demonstrate his inferiority to his alleged master. The fact is, however, that except for *The Man of Feeling,* which bears some structural and stylistic resemblances to *Sentimental Journey,* his writings show little real affinity with Sterne. Mackenzie must be judged on his own merit rather than in the light of his greater contemporaries. His was a minor talent, to be sure, but one deserving of more attention, as I have tried to show, than the limbo to which literary historians have relegated him.

When we forget the historical labels and facile generalizations, *The Man of Feeling* comes to be seen as a carefully wrought novel designed to evoke a wide range of emotional nuances. It is a work of fragile beauty though easily overshadowed by Mackenzie's third novel, upon which his merit as a novelist must ultimately rest. *Julia de Roubigné* represents a significant contribution to the development of the English novel in that it revitalized the complex epistolary technique Richardson had perfected in *Clarissa.* Without falling prey to that writer's prolixity, Mackenzie utilized Richardson's alternate points of view, which complement and contradict each other, to create an enduring work of fiction. We have only to compare *Julia* with Fanny Burney's *Evelina* (1778), where a single point of view predominates, to recognize how rarely Richardson's successors mastered his epistolary form.

Of equal importance are some of Mackenzie's contributions to the *Mirror* and *Lounger.* Mayo has characterized his magazine fiction as "probably the most distinguished since Addison and Steele."[1] Certainly, his three long tales are masterful psychological studies and constitute a major contribution to the evolution of this forerunner of the modern short story. Moving with consummate skill and control, he focuses attention on his protagonists' inner conflicts and conveys his meaning by implication and subtle suggestion. Equal to this creative achievement are the best of his critical papers—the two essays on Shakespeare. While his analysis of Hamlet anticipates Goethe and later influenced A. C. Bradley, his examination of Falstaff, though long overshadowed by Morgann's, is probably the best and most modern eighteenth-century interpretation of Shakespeare's comic knight. Taken together, these essays demonstrate the depth and intuitive grasp of Mackenzie's literary criticism.

If Mackenzie is no longer read, it is due in no small part to our antipathy toward sentimentality, which we are prone to ridicule in our ancestors even when we are blind to it in our contemporaries. Yet, beneath the shell of Mackenzie's emotionalism, there exists an esthetic core worthy of perusal even after two centuries. Though limited in his range and his art, though overshadowed by such contemporaries as Scott and Burns, Mackenzie remains a significant, though minor, figure in the history of Scottish literature.

Notes and References

Chapter One

1. Harold William Thompson, *A Scottish Man of Feeling* (London, 1931), p. 30.
2. *The Anecdotes and Egotisms of Henry Mackenzie*, ed. Harold W. Thompson (London, 1927), p. 63. Hereafter cited as *Anecdotes.*
3. *Ibid.*, p. 16.
4. *Ibid.*, p. 137.
5. *Ibid.*, p. 85.
6. Thompson, p. 31.
7. *Anecdotes*, p. 79.
8. Thompson, p. 55.
9. *Anecdotes*, p. 34.
10. *Ibid.*, p. 194.
11. *Account of the Life and Writings of John Home* (Edinburgh, 1822), p. 38.
12. Thompson, pp. 61–64.
13. *Anecdotes*, pp. 184–85.
14. "Passe-Temps," National Library of Scotland (hereafter cited as N.L.S.), MS 2535, f. 3.
15. Thompson, p. 76.
16. All references to the text of Mackenzie's writings, unless otherwise noted, are to the eight-volume edition of his *Works* (Edinburgh, 1808).
17. Cf. Sir Balaam in Pope's *Epistle to Allen Lord Bathurst*, ll. 339–402.
18. *Henry Mackenzie, Letters to Elizabeth Rose of Kilravock*, ed. Horst W. Drescher, Neue Beiträge zur englischen Philologie, vol 8 (Münster, Westf., 1967), p. 90, n. 3. Hereafter cited as *Letters.*
19. *Anecdotes*, p. 113.
20. *Ibid.*, p. 185.
21. *Ibid.*, pp. 186–87.
22. *Letters*, p. 5, Nov. 26, 1768.
23. *Ibid.*, p. 89, June 17, 1771.
24. Henry Grey Graham, *Scottish Men of Letters in the Eighteenth Century* (London, 1908), p. 417.

25. *Letters,* p. 188, May 13, 1776.

26. *Mirror,* No. 110, V, 79.

27. *Mirror,* No. 1, by George Home. Quotations from *Mirror* and *Lounger* essays not written by Mackenzie are taken from *British Essayists,* ed. A. Chalmers (London, 1823), vols. XXVIII-XXXI.

28. For a definitive study of these two periodicals, see Horst W. Drescher, *Themen und Formen des periodischen Essays im späten 18. Jahrhundert: Untersuchungen zu den schottischen Wochenschriften "The Mirror" und "The Lounger"* (Frankfurt am Main, 1971). This book was published many months after the completion of my own work.

29. Sir Walter Scott, *The Lives of the Novelists* (London, [1928]), p. 301.

30. *Letters,* pp. 137–38. In Letter No. 8 of Brutus, Mackenzie argues that avarice "has changed the sober and moderate economy of domestic life, which nursed at once the private and the patriotic virtues; it has substituted the vanity of ostentatious wealth for the ambition of an honest popularity, and spread over the land the refinements of Eastern luxury, to displace the wholesome enjoyments of industry, and the manly and vigorous exertion of genius." *Letters of Brutus to Certain Celebrated Political Characters* (Edinburgh, 1791), p. 77.

31. Thompson, p. 183.

32. *The Letters of Robert Burns,* ed. J. De Lancey Ferguson, 2 vols. (Oxford, 1931), I, 14.

33. Anon., "Some Account of the Life and Writings of Robert Burns," *Scots Magazine,* LIX (1797), 3.

34. David Daiches, *Robert Burns* (New York, 1950), pp. 108–109.

35. *The Letters of Robert Burns,* I, 57.

36. "Account of the German Theatre," *Transactions of the Royal Society of Edinburgh,* II, pt. 2, set 2 (1790), 180–81.

37. John Gibson Lockhart, *The Life of Sir Walter Scott, Bart.* (London, 1893), pp. 55–56, 68.

38. Thompson, p. 311.

39. *Letters of Brutus,* pp. 1–2.

40. Pierpont Morgan Library, Autograph Letter, Dec. 22, 1802.

41. N.L.S. MS 648, f. 16, transcript of letter.

42. N.L.S. MS 2537, f. 2.

43. Thompson, pp. 377–78.

44. *The Journal of Sir Walter Scott,* ed. W. E. K. Anderson (Oxford, 1972), p. 626.

Chapter Two

1. *Letters*, p. 101, Oct. 9, 1771.
2. David Daiches, *The Paradox of Scottish Culture: The Eighteenth-Century Experience* (London, 1964), p. 77.
3. See, for example, Walter Allen, *The English Novel* (New York, 1958), p. 87; Albert J. Kuhn, Introduction to *Three Sentimental Novels* (New York, 1970), p. xix; Marvin Mudrick, *Jane Austen: Irony as Defense and Discovery* (Berkeley, 1968), p. 10, n. 18.
4. John Rae, *Life of Adam Smith* (1895; rpt. New York, 1965), p. 334. See also Peter W. Clayden, *The Early Life of Samuel Rogers* (London, 1887), pp. 166–67.
5. N.L.S., MS 646, f. 7, 1781, transcript.
6. N.L.S., MS 6387, f. 1.
7. Adam Smith, *The Theory of Moral Sentiments*, 4th ed. (London, 1774), Pt. I, § I, Ch. I, p. 2. Unless otherwise noted, all references are to this edition.
8. *Ibid.*, Ch. V, p. 33.
9. *Ibid.*, Ch. I, p. 2.
10. James Beattie, *Essays on Poetry and Music, as They Affect the Mind* (London, 1779), p. 184.
11. Smith, Pt. I, § I, Ch. I, p. 3.
12. *Ibid.*, Pt. IV, Ch. II, p. 285.
13. "Humanity is the virtue of a woman, generosity of a man." Smith, Pt. IV, Ch. II, p. 285.
14. *Ibid.*, Pt. IV, Ch. II, pp. 285–86.
15. *Ibid.*, Pt. I, § I, Ch. I, p. 5.
16. *Ibid.*, Pt. II, § I, Ch. V, pp. 124–26.
17. *Ibid.*, Pt. III, Ch. II, p. 201.
18. *Ibid.*, p. 221.
19. *Ibid.*, p. 219.
20. *Ibid.*, Ch. III, p. 231.
21. There are, for example, many resemblances between Goldsmith's *The Vicar of Wakefield* (1766) and *The Man of Feeling*. For a comparison of the two novels, see Brian Vickers, Introduction to *The Man of Feeling* (London, 1967), pp. xviii–xxii.
22. On May 9, 1771, Mackenzie wrote to James Elphinston: "I lighted on dhe person ov a curate, becauz dhe curate iz often dhe spoartsman ov dhe parrish; and, amongst curates, I fancy, might ezily be found sevveral such (plump, unfeeling, *good sort ov men*) az dhat logiscian, hoos figgure I hav chanced to bring into' my Introduccion." *Forty Years' Correspondence between Geniusses ov boath Sexes and James Elphinston* (London, 1791–94), I, 263–64; here-

after cited as *Elphinston.* Spelling conforms to Elphinston's *Inglish Orthoggraphy epittomized* (London, 1790).

23. George Meredith, "An Essay on Comedy," in *Comedy*, ed. Wylie Sypher (Garden City, N.Y., 1956), pp. 42, 47.

24. Mackenzie, Ralph E. Jenkins suggests, "must persuade the reader to admire Harley, who at first glance seems to be an impractical, weak and ridiculous character." "The Art of the Theorist: Rhetorical Structure in *The Man of Feeling*," *Studies in Scottish Literature*, IX (1971), 5. This essay came to my attention long after I had completed my own study.

25. Smith, Pt. I, § II, Ch. IV, pp. 63–64.

26. *Anecdotes*, p. 186.

27. *Ibid.*, p. 190. Note his apology to his cousin, after quoting Harley: "Forgive me for so often making Quotations from myself; it does not proceed altogether from vanity, but partly from my writing so much from the immediate Impulse of the Mind, that when the same Sentiments arise, much the same words present themselves to express them.—If my Performances have any Merit, they owe it to this." *Letters*, p. 77, March 23, 1771.

28. Cf. *Letters*, pp. 13, 29; *Elphinston*, I, 263.

29. Henry Cockburn, who knew Mackenzie, described him as "a hard-headed practical man, as full of worldly wisdom as most of his fictitious characters are devoid of it; and this without in the least impairing the affectionate softness of his heart." *Memorials of his Time* (New York, 1856), p. 252.

30. David G. Spencer, "Henry Mackenzie, a Practical Sentimentalist," *Papers on Language & Literature*, III (1967), 318.

31. As he writes to his cousin: "I have been at war with the World from a Boy." *Letters*, p. 34, Jan. 6, 1770.

32. Dale Kramer, "The Structural Unity of *The Man of Feeling*," *Studies in Short Fiction*, I (1964), 193.

33. *Elphinston*, I, 215.

34. *The Man of Feeling*, Sir Walter Scott points out, "is in fact no narrative, but a series of successive incidents, each rendered interesting by the mode in which they operate on the feelings of Harley." *The Lives of the Novelists*, p. 298.

35. *Letters*, p. 16, July 8, 1769.

36. "Passe-Temps," N.L.S., MS 2535, ff. 92–93.

37. *Elphinston*, I, 169; *Letters*, p. 5.

38. "Passe-Temps," N.L.S., MS 2535, f. 95.

39. *Ibid.*, ff. 93–94. Likewise, "Lavinia, A Pastoral" (I, 211–15) is to be found in ff. 77–79, written in 1766.

40. Northrop Frye, *Anatomy of Criticism* (1957; rpt. New York, 1966), p. 309.
41. Vickers, pp. xvi–xviii.
42. *Letters*, pp. 35–36, Jan. 24, 1770.
43. *Letters*, p. 29, Nov. 29, 1769.
44. René Wellek, *A History of Modern Criticism: 1750–1950* (New Haven, 1955), I, 124.
45. As Mrs. Barbauld suggests in her "Inquiry into those kinds of distress which excite agreeable sensations" (1773), "misfortunes which excite pity must not be too horrid and overwhelming. The mind is rather stunned than softened by great calamities." *Works* (New York, 1826), II, 49.
46. "Those who have touched the springs of pity with the finest hand, have mingled light strokes of pleasantry and mirth in their most pathetic passages." *Ibid.*, II, 55.
47. *Ibid.*, II, 51.
48. Alexander Gerard, *Essay on Taste*, 3rd ed. (1780; rpt. Gainesville, Florida, 1963), pp. 79–80.
49. Hannah More, "Sensibility," in *Works* (New York, 1835), V, 379.
50. Anon., "The Birth of Sensibility," *London Magazine*, XLV (1776), 195.
51. Hugh Blair, *Lectures on Rhetoric and Belles Lettres* (1783) (Halifax, 1850), Lect. XLV, p. 628.
52. At least nine editions of *The Man of Feeling* had been published by 1800. Harold Thompson, *A Scottish Man of Feeling*, pp. 417–18.
53. Anon., *Monthly Review*, XLIV (1771), 418.
54. *Elphinston*, I, 258.
55. *The Private Letter-Books of Sir Walter Scott*, ed. Wilfred Partington (London, 1930), 273.
56. Thompson, p. 170.
57. William Roberts, *Memoirs of The Life and Correspondence of Mrs. Hannah More*, 4 vols. (London, 1835), I, 143–44.
58. *The Private Letter-Books of Sir Walter Scott*, p. 273.
59. David Hume, *A Treatise of Human Nature* (London, 1923), II, 127.

Chapter Three

1. Anon., *London Magazine*, XLII (1773), 149.
2. *Letters*, p. 125, March 1, 1773.
3. *Anecdotes*, p. 189.
4. *Elphinston*, I, 263.

5. Lumley, Sindall's tutor, exhibits similar traits (I, 330–31, 342).

6. Note Mackenzie's explanation of Jack Ryland's gullibility: "he was guiltless of imputing to others, what his honesty never experienced in himself" (II, 71).

7. Adam Smith, *Theory of Moral Sentiments* (London, 1869), Pt. III, Ch. II, p. 105. Smith added this passage in the revised 6th ed. (1790).

8. A. L. Macfie, *The Individual in Society: Papers on Adam Smith* (London, 1967), pp. 83–84.

9. *Ibid.*, p. 87.

10. Smith, Pt. V, Ch. II, p. 304. Cf. "Fashion may be also considered as pow'rful in the Formation of Manners: from a Regard to *Appearance* is deriv'd the Source of most actions in a certain Rank." "Passe-Temps," N.L.S. MS 2535, f. 99.

11. Smith, Pt. II, § II, Ch. II, pp. 143–44.

12. *Ibid.*, Pt. I, § I, Ch. V, p. 30.

13. *Ibid.*, Pt. V, Ch. II, p. 313.

14. *Ibid.*, pp. 317–18.

15. *Ibid.*, p. 313.

16. *Ibid.*, p. 315.

Chapter Four

1. Sir Walter Scott, *Lives of the Novelists*, pp. 299–300.

2. Henry Home, Lord Kames, *Elements of Criticism* (New York, 1844), p. 415.

3. J. M. S. Tompkins, *The Popular Novel in England, 1770–1800* (1932; rpt. Lincoln, Nebraska, 1961), p. 333.

4. *Letters*, p. 199, Jan. 27, 1777. Cf. *Lounger*, No. 64.

5. In Rousseau's novel, her father's tears overcome Julie's reluctance to marry Wolmar.

6. Francis Hutcheson, "Illustrations upon the Moral Sense" (1728), in *British Moralists*, ed. L. A. Selby-Bigge (1897; rpt. Indianapolis, 1964), I, 413.

7. In "A Soliloquy," a poem written in 1764, Mackenzie argues that "the least feeling, least of misery knows" (VIII, 22).

8. *Letters*, p. 184, December 18, 1775.

9. *Ibid.*, p. 139, August 6, 1773.

10. Cf. Adam Smith's analysis of social cooperation: "We address ourselves, not to their [men's] humanity but to their self-love, and never talk to them of our own necessities but of their advantages." See also his criticism of slavery: "The experience of all ages and nations, I believe, demonstrates that work done by slaves, though it

appears to cost only their maintenance, is in the end the dearest of any. A person who can acquire no property, can have no other interest but to eat as much, and to labour as little as possible." *Wealth of Nations*, 1776 (London, 1925), I, 16, 364.

11. *Letters*, p. 134, May 21, 1773.

12. Cf. Henry Home, Lord Kames, *Sketches of the History of Man* (Edinburgh, 1774), Bk. I, Sk. VII, pp. 255–56.

13. *Lounger*, No. 100, VII, 25.

Chapter Five

1. *Account of the Life and Writings of John Home*, pp. 93–94.

2. J. M. S. Tompkins, *The Popular Novel in England*, p. 343.

3. *Letters*, pp. 141–42, October 20, 1773.

4. Leigh Hunt, *Classic Tales, Serious and Lively: With Critical Essays on the Merits and Reputations of the Authors* (London, 1806–07), I, 7.

5. Robert D. Mayo, *The English Novel in the Magazines, 1740–1815* (Evanston, 1962), pp. 256–57.

6. *Ibid.*, p. 597.

7. P. 21.

8. See Gerard A. Barker, "Henry Mackenzie's Adaptation of Lillo's *Fatal Curiosity*," *Bulletin of the New York Public Library*, LXXIV (1970), 544–46.

9. Emendation based upon N.L.S. MS 647, f. 10.

10. *Letters*, p. 47, June 2, 1770.

11. Note the portrait of Lentulus, another "Man of Feeling," in *The Pursuits of Happiness*: "With knowledge just to guide, but not perplex; / That ne'er at truth's plain dictates took offence; / That ne'er in subtilty was lost to sense;" (VIII, 87).

12. *Letters*, p. 74, March 10, 1771.

13. Jean Francois Marmontel, *Moral Tales* (London, 1781), pp. 175–90.

14. *Ibid.*, pp. 182–83.

15. Mayo, p. 573.

16. *Anecdotes*, pp. 189–90. Cf. abbreviated version in N.L.S. MS 2537, f. 7v.

17. *Anecdotes*, p. 232.

Chapter Six

1. *Anecdotes*, p. 187; *Letters*, p. 10.

2. *Virginia; or, The Roman Father. A Tragedy*, privately printed

1824?, n.p., British Museum copy, C. 58, f. 2. Quoted by permission of the B.M.

3. *Ibid.*, p. [2].

4. Titus Livius, *History of Rome* (1922; rpt. Cambridge, Mass., 1967), II, 147.

5. *Ibid.*, II, 145.

6. *Anecdotes*, p. 187.

7. Voltaire, "Essays upon the Manners and Spirit of Nations, and upon the Principal Facts of History, from Charlemagne to Louis XIII," in *Works* (Paris, 1901), XXIV, 179–81.

8. Harold Thompson, *A Scottish Man of Feeling*, p. 165. For confirmation that Mackenzie was in London at the beginning of 1773, see *Letters*, p. 123.

9. Morgan Library, Autograph Letter to Dr. Currie.

10. *Letters*, p. 109, Feb. 19, 1772.

11. In his letter to Dr. Currie, he claims that, when he wrote *The Spanish Father*, he "was not sufficiently aware of the difficulty of writing a Tragedy." Morgan Library, Autograph Letter.

12. René Wellek, *A History of Modern Criticism*, I, 118.

13. Lord Kames, *Elements of Criticism*, p. 417.

14. *Ibid.*, p. 415.

15. Morgan Library, Autograph Letter.

16. *Letters*, p. 125.

17. *Anecdotes*, p. 208. See also *Letters*, p. 76.

18. A first edition of 1,000 copies of *The Prince of Tunis* was sold out in Edinburgh within two weeks. *Scots Magazine*, XXXV (1773), 144–47; *Letters*, p. 128.

19. *Letters*, p. 126, March 1, 1773.

20. *Letters*, p. 130, April 9, 1773.

21. William Robertson, *History of the Reign of the Emperor Charles V* (Philadelphia, 1864), II, 255–58.

22. *Ibid.*, II, 257.

23. *Anecdotes*, p. 162.

24. *Ibid.*, p. 208.

25. *London Stage, 1660–1800*, Pt. 5, ed. Charles B. Hogan (Carbondale, Ill., 1968), II, 1211–12.

26. "Cumberland led me to believe that it did not meet with justice in the acting of the principal character, of which it was difficult to bring out the little shades, the *nuances*, as the French call them." *Anecdotes*, p. 207. Writing to Leclerc de Septchenes on Jan. 28, 1788, Mackenzie complains: "The Theatre is occupied by comic operas or rather farces set to music; yet so much are the[y] in vogue

that *Covent Garden* where they are play'd is always full, while Drury Lane with Mrs. Siddons and several other of the best performers is so empty that at a late meeting of the proprietors it was seriously debated whether it should not be shut up." N.L.S. MS 573, f. 85, transcript.

27. Huntington Library, HM LA 852.

28. Cf. *Lounger*, No. 19, written by Fraser Tytler.

29. Charles H. Gray, *Theatrical Criticism in London to 1795* (New York, 1931), pp. 253–54.

30. Huntington Library, HM LA 852, l. 27; only the first sentence appears in *False Shame*.

31. J. M. S. Tompkins, *The Popular Novel in England*, pp. 80–83.

32. *Lounger*, No. 85; see also *Mirror*, Nos. 38 & 40, by Mackenzie, No. 35, Pt. 1, by David Hume (the philosopher's nephew). Ironically enough, Lord Chesterfield himself condemns fear of ridicule. See *Letters to his Son, Philip Stanhope, Esq.*, 6th ed. (London, 1775), II, 138–39.

33. *Letters*, p. 74, March 10, 1771. Cf. *Works*, I, 151–52.

34. Huntington Library, HM LA 852, lv. 50–51.

Chapter Seven

1. Robert Mayo, *The English Novel in the Magazines*, pp. 141–42.

2. *Lounger*, No. 20, June 18, 1785 (V, 176–87).

3. *Ibid.*, p. 146; Harold Thompson, *A Scottish Man of Feeling*, pp. 204–205.

4. *Letters*, p. 14, July 8, 1769.

5. *Anecdotes*, p. 156.

6. *Lounger*, Nos. 64 & 90, by Mackenzie; *Mirror*, Nos. 10 & 47, by William Craig; *Lounger*, No. 74, by Alexander Abercromby.

7. Cf. "Account of the German Theatre," pp. 165, 167.

8. "The term *sentiment* is appropriated to such thoughts as are prompted by passion." Lord Kames, *Elements of Criticism*, p. 483.

9. Erik Erämetsä, *A Study of the Word "Sentimental" and of other Linguistic Characteristics of Eighteenth Century Sentimentalism in England* (Helsinki, 1951), pp. 57–58.

10. Anon., Review of *An Essay on Sensibility*, *Critical Review*, LXVIII (1789), 447.

11. Cf. Clara Reeve, *The Progress of Romance* (1785; rpt. New York, 1930), I, 139.

12. Robert Chambers, *A Biographical Dictionary of Eminent Scotsmen*, 4 vols. (London, 1864), III, 517.

13. *Lounger*, Nos. 27–28, Aug. 6 & 13, 1785 (V, 221–46).

14. John Dryden, "Heads of an Answer to Rymer," in *John Dryden: Selected Criticism* (Oxford, 1970), p. 144.

15. Joseph Addison, *Spectator*, No. 39 (London, 1753), I, 157.

16. Lord Kames, *Elements of Criticism*, p. 416.

17. Hugh Blair, *Lectures on Rhetoric and Belles Lettres*, Lect. XLV, p. 617.

18. *Ibid.*, p. 616.

19. "In all that relates to practice, there is no man who seriously means to persuade another, but addresses himself to his passions more or less; for this plain reason, that passions are the great springs of human action." *Ibid.*, Lect. XXXII, p. 433.

20. *Ibid.*, Lect. XLV, p. 616.

21. *Ibid.*, Lect. XLVI, p. 634.

22. Cf. Addison, *Spectator*, No. 39.

23. Lord Kames, *Elements of Criticism*, p. 417.

24. *Ibid.*, p. 415.

25. Blair, Lect. XLV, p. 617.

26. ". . . no evil is so pernicious as that which grows in the soil from which good should have sprung" (I, 283).

27. As Reverend Annesly admonishes, "in the more important articles of belief or conviction, let not the flow of ridicule be mistaken for the force of argument" (I, 296).

28. Stuart M. Tave, *The Amiable Humorist* (Chicago, 1960), pp. 35–39. E.g., Lord Kames, *Elements of Criticism*, pp. 183–84; James Boswell, *Hypochondriak*, No. 62, *Boswell's Column* (London, 1951), pp. 313–18.

29. Anthony, Earl of Shaftesbury, *Characteristics of Men, Manners, Opinions, Times, etc.* (1900; rpt. Gloucester, Mass., 1963), I, 9–15, 85–86.

30. *Letters*, p. 187, May 13, 1776.

31. *Anecdotes*, p. 201.

32. A. C. Bradley, *Shakespeare Tragedy* (London, 1905), pp. 91–92. Ernest Tuveson, "The Importance of Shaftesbury," *ELH*, XX (1953), 293–94.

33. Paul S. Conklin, *A History of Hamlet Criticism, 1601–1821* (New York, 1947), p. 67.

34. Samuel Johnson, *Notes to Shakespeare* (Augustan Reprint; Los Angeles, 1958), III, 182.

35. William Richardson, *A Philosophical Analysis and Illustration of Some of Shakespeare's Remarkable Characters* (London, 1774), pp. 118–19.

36. Mackenzie, in turn, influenced Richardson's second essay on

Hamlet, *Essays on Shakespeare's Dramatic Characters* (1784). See Robert W. Babcock, *The Genesis of Shakespeare Idolatry, 1766–1799* (Chapel Hill, N.C., 1931), p. 150.

37. *The Journal of Sir Walter Scott*, p. 26.

38. *Letters*, p. 173, July 20, 1775.

39. Johann Wolfgang von Goethe, *Wilhelm Meister* (London, 1930), I, 212.

40. Bradley, p. 91.

41. *Ibid.*, pp. 113, 116–17.

42. Cf. Samuel Johnson's description: "Thou compound of sense and vice; of sense which may be admired, but not esteemed, of vice which may be despised, but hardly detested." *Notes to Shakespeare*, II, Pt. I, 57.

43. Maurice Morgann, "Essay on the Dramatic Character of Sir John Falstaff" (1777), in *Eighteenth Century Essays on Shakespeare*, ed. D. Nicol Smith (1903; rpt. New York, 1962), p. 220.

44. Mackenzie's interpretation depends on a successful Falstaff whose schemes prosper and who outwits his opponents. Once he is defeated, as at the end of *2 Henry IV*, once he becomes a comic butt, as in *The Merry Wives of Windsor*, he loses much of his nonchalance and good humor.

45. Benedetto Croce, *Ariosto, Shakespeare and Corneille* (New York, 1920), p. 215.

46. Franz Alexander, "A Note on Falstaff," *Psychoanalytic Quarterly*, II (1933), 598–99.

47. R. F. Brissenden, "Authority, Guilt, and Anxiety in *The Theory of Moral Sentiments*," *Texas Studies in Literature and Language*, XI (1969), 949–51. See also A. L. Macfie, *The Individual in Society: Papers on Adam Smith*, p. 80, n. 61.

48. Adam Smith, *Moral Sentiments*, Pt. III, Ch. II, p. 198.

49. *Ibid.*

50. Mackenzie's analysis seems far more perceptive and sound than Morgann's labored attempt to prove Falstaff "cowardly in appearance and brave in reality," p. 146.

51. Smith, *Moral Sentiments*, Pt. III, Ch. I, pp. 193–95.

52. Addison, *Spectator*, No. 62, I, 249. Locke speaks of wit making up "pleasant pictures, and agreeable visions." *Essay Concerning Human Understanding* (London, 1788), I, 143.

53. Thomas Whately, "Remarks on some of the Characters of Shakespeare" (1785), in *Shakespeare Criticism, 1623–1840*, ed. D. Nicol Smith (1916; rpt. London, 1963), p. 125.

54. *Ibid.*, p. 129.

55. *Ibid.*, p. 138.

56. Coleridge, in his "Lectures of 1811–12," makes a similar comparison of Falstaff, Richard III, and Iago: "characters of complete moral depravity, but of first-rate wit and talents." *Coleridge's Shakespearean Criticism*, ed. T. M. Raysor (Cambridge, Mass., 1930), II, 29–30; see also II, 181.

57. Whately, p. 127.

58. *Ibid.*, p. 144.

59. Richardson, pp. 74–75.

60. Walter J. Bate, *From Classic to Romantic: Premises of Taste in Eighteenth-Century England* (New York, 1961), pp. 131–32. See also M. A. Goldberg, *Smollett and the Scottish School* (Albuquerque, N.M., 1959), pp. 53–54.

61. Dugald Stewart, *Elements of the Philosophy of the Human Mind* (Edinburgh, 1792), p. 502, quoted by Walter J. Bate, "The Sympathetic Imagination in Eighteenth-Century English Criticism," *ELH*, XII (1945), p. 148.

Chapter Eight

1. Robert Mayo, *The English Novel in the Magazines*, p. 124.

Selected Bibliography

PRIMARY SOURCES

1. Manuscripts

The National Library of Scotland contains most of Mackenzie's extant correspondence and papers, including the manuscripts of *Anecdotes and Egotisms* and "Passe-Temps," as well as unpublished essays and reviews. *The Force of Fashion* manuscript, submitted to the Lord Chamberlain, is in the Larpent Collection (HM LA 852) of Huntington Library.

2. Letters

Henry Mackenzie, Letters to Elizabeth Rose of Kilravock. Ed. Horst W. Drescher. Neue Beiträge zur englischen Philologie, vol. 8. Műnster, West Germany: Aschendorff, 1967.

Forty Years' Correspondence between Geniusses ov Boath Sexes, and James Elphinston. 6 vols. London: W. Ritchardson, 1791–94.

3. Works by Henry Mackenzie

Works of Henry Mackenzie. 8 vols. Edinburgh: A. Constable, 1808. The standard edition, with notes and corrections by the author.

The Shipwreck; or, Fatal Curiosity. London: T. Cadell, 1784.

"Account of the German Theatre." *Transactions of the Royal Society of Edinburgh*, II, pt. 2, set 2 (1790), 154–92.

Letters of Brutus to Certain Celebrated Political Characters. Edinburgh: Stewart, Ruthuen & Co., 1791.

Account of the Life and Writings of John Home. Edinburgh: A. Constable, 1822.

Virginia; or, The Roman Father. A Tragedy. Privately printed, 1824? British Museum copy, C. 58, f. 2.

Anecdotes and Egotisms of Henry Mackenzie. Ed. Harold W. Thompson. London: Oxford University Press, 1927.

The Man of Feeling. Ed. Brian Vickers. London: Oxford University Press, 1967. Based on revised second edition, includes good introduction, bibliography, and notes.

SECONDARY SOURCES

BAKER, ERNEST A. *The History of the English Novel.* Vol. V. London: H. F. & G. Witherby, 1934. Includes a detailed but often misleading discussion of Mackenzie.

BARKER, GERARD A. "Henry Mackenzie's Adaptation of Lillo's *Fatal Curiosity.*" *Bulletin of the New York Public Library,* LXXIV (1970), 532–48. Examines significance of changes made in Lillo's play.

BRYANT, BYRON R. "The Fiction of Henry Mackenzie." Unpublished doctoral dissertation, Stanford University, 1955. Perceptive and appreciative analysis of Mackenzie's novels.

HUNT, LEIGH, ed. *Classic Tales, Serious and Lively: With Critical Essays on the Merits and Reputations of the Authors.* Vol. I. London: Hunt & Reynell, 1806–07. Acclaims Mackenzie as writer of tales.

KRAMER, DALE. "The Structural Unity of *The Man of Feeling.*" *Studies in Short Fiction,* I (1964), 191–99. Argues for a thematic organization, based upon education of hero.

MAYO, ROBERT D. *The English Novel in the Magazines, 1740–1815.* Evanston: Northwestern University Press, 1962. Contains an excellent discussion of Mackenzie's significance as a periodical essayist.

ROUCH, JOHN S. "Henry Mackenzie: A Re-examination." Unpublished doctoral dissertation, University of Cincinnati, 1961. Argues for a pervasive moral dualism in Mackenzie but overextends thesis.

SPENCER, DAVID G. "Henry Mackenzie, a Practical Sentimentalist." *Papers on Language and Literature,* III (1967), 314–26. Useful, perceptive reassessment of Mackenzie's first two novels.

SCOTT, SIR WALTER. *The Lives of the Novelists.* London: J. M. Dent, [1928]. Includes a highly sympathetic, influential critique of Mackenzie.

THOMPSON, HAROLD W. *A Scottish Man of Feeling: Some Account of Henry Mackenzie, Esq. of Edinburgh and of the Golden Age of Burns and Scott.* London: Oxford University Press, 1931. The standard biographical and critical study of Mackenzie. Indispensable for its wealth of information; occasionally misleading in its criticism.

TOMPKINS, J. M. S. *The Popular Novel in England, 1770–1800.* Lincoln, Nebraska: University of Nebraska Press, 1961. Contains brief but perceptive discussions of Mackenzie's novels.

Index